D0930480

DAVID JANSSEN
My Fugitive

DAVID JANSSEN
My Fugitive

by

ELLIE JANSSEN

as told to by
J.D. Michael Phelps

LIFETIME BOOKS, INC.
2131 Hollywood Blvd., Suite 305
Hollywood, FL 33020

This publication is designed to provide accurate and authoritative information in regard to the subject matter covered. It is sold with the understanding that the publisher is not engaged in rendering legal, accounting, or other professional service. If legal advice or other assistance is required, the services of a competent professional person should be sought. *From A Declaration of Principles jointly adopted by a Committee of the American Bar Association and a Committee of Publishers.*

Library of Congress Cataloging-in-Publication Data

Janssen, Ellie.
    David Janssen, my fugitive / by Ellie Janssen, as told to J.D. Michael Phelps.
        p.   cm.
    ISBN 0-8119-0797-X : $18.95
    1. Janssen, David.   2. Janssen, Ellie.   3. Actors   United States   Biography.   I. Phelps, J. D. Michael. II. Title.
    PN2287.J36J35   1994
    791.45'028'092--dc20
    [B]   94-24713
                                                                CIP

Dedication

I never considered the difficulties I would experience when I began this book. I kept going in spite of some painful and haunting memories. I also reveled in so many, many warm and good memories of my life with a great man. I feel this book is necessary for his loving fans, to know the truth, to know the real David Janssen.

David would be enormously pleased to see that Harrison Ford has brought the character of Dr. Richard Kimble, "The Fugitive," and his search for justice, to the minds of millions of people once again.

What has been satisfying to me, and what would have made David secretly happy (although he probably wouldn't have shown it), is that even now so many people still remember and celebrate the original Dr. Richard Kimble that they have a national convention every year to commemorate him.

Even so, with all the fame "The Fugitive" movies are bringing to Dr. Kimble, I wanted to make sure that David continued to be remembered and was given his proper place in the entertainment industry. Thank you from my deepest feelings for remembering David Janssen so long, and so lovingly.

ELLIE JANSSEN
NOVEMBER 1994

Contents

Acknowledgments

There have been so many kind and generous people, our friends who have helped me put this book together, far too many to name on this page, but each knows I am very grateful for their time and loving support.

I do want to express here my special thanks to Berniece Dalton Janssen, David's mother, for all her contributions. To Fran Caldwell for her many hours of help and to our Editor, David Kohn of Deerfield Beach, Florida, for his masterful work and patience in helping us meet our deadline.

To the members of the various David Janssen and Fans of the Fugitive clubs, worldwide, please see the back of the book.

ELLIE JANSSEN
NOVEMBER 1994

I wish to give special thanks to my attorney, Frank X. Gliozzo, of Coral Gables, Florida and his Administrative Assistants, Alicia Ramos and Stephanie Slater. With their help this book was finalized. Special thanks to my godson, Attorney Miguel A. Rodez, of Coral Gables, for his support and contributions.

J.D. MICHAEL PHELPS
NOVEMBER 1994

FOREWORD

Ellie and David Janssen were married on August 23, 1958 in Las Vegas Nevada. David was starring in his first television series, *Richard Diamond–Private Detective*.

Their love and happiness grew, nurtured by their constant support for each other. They were inseparable.

On their tenth wedding anniversary, David shocked Ellie by telling her he was leaving her for a Hollywood starlet.

After months of agonizing, hoping against hope that David would come to his senses and return to their marital home, Ellie filed for dissolution of marriage.

With their marriage ended by a judge's order on August 27, 1970, Ellie made efforts to structure her life without David. She has traveled around the world, and today lives in Brentwood, Los Angeles.

I convinced Ellie to write this book, commencing in 1987. David had died in February of 1980. It is apparent to me, and all who know Ellie, that her love for David has never died. Writing this book has been both painful and cathartic for Ellie. There is much more to tell, but we have endeavored to bring to David's millions of fans the most important facts of David's life and their life together. Contrary to the tabloids' reports, Ellie has told the truth for the benefit of his fans.

MIKE PHELPS
NOVEMBER 1994

FOREWORD

CHAPTER I

"The past is prologue." – WILLIAM SHAKESPEARE
And it is with the past I must begin...

LAS VEGAS, NEVADA — November, 1955

The airliner glided gracefully out of the early November sky onto the runway at McCarran Field. A few minutes later, I stepped out onto the tarmac and toward a new life. Thousands of sparkling stars, rarely visible in the New York sky I had left behind, twinkled from the blackness overhead.

During the flight, I had mixed feelings: the tug of separation from my daughters, combined with loneliness and fear of the unknown. On the approach to the Las Vegas airport, these emotions yielded to a rising sense of excitement as I looked out the window of the aircraft at the lights of the Oasis in the Desert. It seemed a million lights of every hue were stabbing their fingers into the sky, then crooking them, seemingly to entice me.

"Come to my pleasures," they said. "Forget your burdens, your everyday tedium. Come live in fantasy for awhile."

I paused in the terminal long enough to claim my luggage. Hailing a cab, I directed the driver, "El Rancho Hotel." In November, 1955, the Las Vegas "strip" was in its embryonic stage. There was the El Rancho Hotel & Casino, the Flamingo Hotel & Casino, the Desert Inn, the Sands Hotel & Casino, and only a couple of others. All had huge gambling casinos and top-name entertainers in their plush supper clubs and lounges.

I had left New York with only the laws of Nevada as my destination. I was in a highly emotional state of mind, a combination of hurt, anger and confusion. I had no hotel reservations and to my surprise, there were no rooms available. I pleaded with the desk clerk for a room. Friendly and courteous as he tried to be, he could offer me no help.

Standing nearby was Carl Cohen, a top executive of the El Rancho Hotel, who was preparing to join Jakey Friedman as a shareholder and senior executive of the Sands Hotel & Casino. Sympathetically, he noted my distress. He approached me while holding out his hand and introduced himself. He asked where I was from, whether I had ever been to Las Vegas and how long I intended to stay. I was embarrassed when I divulged I would have to be there six weeks.

"I'm here to get a divorce, you see," I told him, my face flushing.

Nevada is a barren state, with the good sense to attract revenue as it can by accepting human realities as they are. Side by side with the gambling and tourist industry was a lesser, but nonetheless lucrative one: divorce. The state required six weeks to establish residency. Once residency was validated, a divorce could be had in a matter of days. Nevada laws at the time allowed the quickest divorces in the country.

Carl, being the very kind and considerate man he was, assured me all would be fine. He made a telephone call and shortly after, a room was provided for me at the Sands.

Over the next few months, we would become good friends. I settled into the room, which was unusually large and quite comfortable. I unpacked and realized that either I had brought too many suitcases or the closets were too small, but, after all, I had to be there six weeks. It was almost two A.M. The late hour plus jet lag, had left me exhausted. I took my shower and collapsed into a restless sleep.

Within a few days I met Eleanor and Beverly Roth, who also befriended me and would become close and lasting friends. Eleanor was the private secretary to Jack Entratter, vice president of entertainment of the Copa Room and lounges at the Sands. Jack had earlier directed the entertainment successes at the Copacabana in New York. He was right at home with this assignment.

From its genesis as a resort phenomenon, Las Vegas has beckoned to the playfulness in us all. Its blandishments have been gambling, the best entertainment talents, extravagant floor shows featuring riveting expanses of near-naked female beauty and very, very good food at reasonable prices. Close by is the desert, Lake Mead, the awesome mass of the Hoover Dam, and the feeling of the Old West, albeit one in which the omnipresent bandits are one-armed. It seems appropriate that a lady, on her way to fall in love with a man whose fame would flower through four years of chasing a human one-armed bandit on network television, should pause here.

Eleanor and Beverly Roth were two of my strongest supporters during this critical period of my life. They taught me how to relax, to enjoy life in Las Vegas, and how to accept my mission there as just another hurdle in life that I would clear. My daughters were being well-attended in New York. Between boarding their school and my family, I would speak with or hear about them several times a week, so I knew all was well. I was calming down and settling into the Las Vegas lifestyle. Fortunately, I never became a gambler. A little blackjack was enough for me.

One morning Eleanor and I were walking through the Sands when a familiar-looking man approached us. He greeted Eleanor warmly and, before she could say a word and while I was trying to recall where I had seen him before, he reached for my hand. He bowed, kissed my fingertips, looked up at me and, with a twinkle in his big, blue eyes said: "I love you." What a wonderful feeling. Then Eleanor interjected with a proper introduction. And that is how I met Frank Sinatra.

Coming to Las Vegas feeling as though I was a failure as a wife and as a woman, had been shattering to my ego. Yet here was one of the most famous and eligible men in the world, telling me he LOVED me at first sight. He made me feel wonderful, even if he didn't mean it.

Frank invited us to his opening show and dinner that evening in the Copa Room. He was just starting a long engagement at the Sands. We accepted graciously.

I went to my salon appointment. I had my hair styled, a manicure and a pedicure.

Then I returned to my room to prepare for the exciting evening ahead.

I learned the early 1950s had been a time of severe trial for Frank Sinatra. Approaching his midthirties, he had just been divorced from Ava Gardner, and his career was threatened by throat trouble. Up to that point, his voice was his career.

But Frank is a fighter. To stay alive professionally, he cajoled and begged for the role of "Maggio" in "From Here To Eternity." He won. He also gave the part a classic portrayal. In 1953, the Motion Picture Academy of Arts and Sciences rewarded Frank's courage and talents by awarding him an Oscar.

He had beaten his throat problem and by November 1955, his career was soaring anew. If there was a cloud in his life, it would have to have been his divorce from Ava. But, on balance, life for Frank Sinatra was better than good.

That evening Eleanor and I were ushered into the Copa Room and seated at a front row, center table. We enjoyed a cocktail and a lovely dinner during the opening act. By the time Frank came on stage, the waiters had removed all the table settings except the cocktails. The room, which had been sold out for Frank's show, fell silent as he walked onto the stage. He seemed to beam his act straight at me. Romantic lyrics wrapped in his fabled phrasing caressed the room, but his eyes seemed to say they were just for me. Seduction by serenade.

His show finished, Frank invited Eleanor and me to join him at his table in the lounge. We eagerly accepted. It was a fun evening. During its course, Frank slipped the key of his suite to Eleanor, asking her to pass it on to me to be used for a more private rendezvous later in the night. When Eleanor took me to the ladies room and told me, I was astounded. My firm message to Frank was a "No, thank you!".

There was no aura of prudery in me, nor was I given to fits of deep introspection or self-justification. The night had certainly been romantic. Maybe it was the second hand invitation, maybe it was that the approach was just a bit rushed. Whatever, my answer was a simple no. Eleanor was a bit more adventuresome. Slipping quietly across the street to her apartment, she gathered her sexiest baby doll nightie and went calling. "Why waste a beautiful suite, an exciting man, and the night's erotic warmup," she thought.

I ran into Frank in the lobby the next afternoon. He kissed my hand again, looked in my eyes and said:

"How could you?"

"How could I what?" I responded.

He then told me about Eleanor's little caprice. We both laughed. I had no idea she would do that. He again invited me to his show and dinner. Of course, I accepted.

I selected a new evening gown, royal blue, low cut back, with small diamond earrings and a matching necklace and gold bracelet. When Frank joined us, he complimented my tastes, telling me how beautiful and stunning I looked. His compliments were always carefully chosen and sincere. His words warmed my heart.

Frank gave me a standing invitation to be his guest at both his shows each evening. Our acquaintance mellowed into friendship within a week or so, and I became very comfortable with him. It was fate that we would become lovers. One evening soon after, Frank and I sat through his usual period of unwinding after the last show with the usual happy people gathered around his tables. Then, earlier than usual, Frank stood took my hand and we ducked out and went directly to his suite.

Music was playing softly in the background as we entered the room. Frank was every woman's dream, determined to please, and he did.

From that night, it seemed that I had ceased being an amused spectator at the fantasy. Instead I became part of it. And, for all the remaining days of my life, I had walked into an entirely new and exciting way of life. It has been said that marriage has ruined many a beautiful romance. My amiable affair with Frank Sinatra would not be so fated. I never fell in love with Frank, nor do I feel he did with me. I never believed we would even consider marriage. There was no deep probing into pasts or psyche searches; we had few expectations, no demands. I think Frank accepted our ties in a similarly objective vein.

We were comfortable together, had fun together. We were just great companions. And because Frank and I both had recently ended unsuccessful and hurtful unions, it may have been mutual wisdom that we settled for what we had, while we played together and made love, we also healed together. We both needed that. I can honestly say to this day, there is a special place, a special love, in my heart for Frank Sinatra.

It was exciting. Frank's magnetism electrified any room he entered. He had charisma. It was more than that and still is. People who deal in entertainment talent know that superstars have some special quality beyond the talent that sets them above the rest. It is indefinable, and it is theirs alone. That probably says it about as clearly as I can about him. Frank Sinatra is — FRANK SINATRA — an original. For me, he was life, energetic and stimulating. Being with him was always exciting and challenging, emotionally and physically.

I had been accustomed to wealth and status before I met Frank. Although my soon-to-be former husband's income may not have matched Frank's, there was plenty. Millions. Very little of that would be mine now, for I had quietly accepted the modest financial terms stipulated by my husband's attorney. I enjoyed the fine homes, tasteful furnishings, plush restaurants and first class travel amenities which money affords people. But the lives and drives of Eastern moneyed people were centered on business. The pace was fast, and business was underlying every social gathering.

Business is money and business comes first — even before wives and families. It was constricting and artificial, in a refined way. One could never forget propriety. Dress right, speak carefully, laugh with restraint, act properly. It was all so stifling. Just once, when someone spilled a drink on someone else, I wanted to hear an emphatic, spontaneous; "Oh, damn it!" But I never did.

There was nothing stifling about being with Frank Sinatra. From my very first acceptance of his invitation to share his table in the lounge after the show, I could tell that this was a very different social set than I had known on the East Coast. Frank's table was actually five tables pushed together across the rear of the lounge. Nothing less would accommodate the entourage which gathered nightly. It commanded an unobstructed view of the entire room and the colorful panoply which consisted of Las Vegas night people.

If I were to paint it, the eye would conjure up King Henry VIII at a royal feast. The parade of chancellors, courtiers and court jesters was constant, yet ever-changing. If they were entertaining in town, or available between appearances or films, the clan's regulars, Dean Martin, Sammy Davis, Jr., Peter Lawford, Joey Bishop and Nelson Riddle, were in attendance during my early times with Frank. All stars in their own right, they were the ones with whom Frank shared close and real friendships.

But I remember somewhat more vividly those who shared in Frank's professional success, those who worked to help Frank become a star and stay on top. Hank Sanicola, his longtime manager, was usually around, as were Jimmy Van Heusen, whose songs graced lovers and solaced losers, and Jilly Rizzo, his longtime friend and sort-of-body-guard. Jilly, the famous restaurateur known on both coasts, was ever-mindful of anyone who was uninvited intruding on Frank's privacy in public, and Jilly kept them at a polite distance. While Frank's star shone brightest, Nelson Riddle's subtle stringed arrangements provided the rich background which so effectively set off its brilliance. And, from every major hotel in Las Vegas, numerous headliners dropped by Frank's table to join in the fun.

Each evening the cast of characters gathered, the players shifting, but the mood constant. Every night was like New Year's Eve at Frank's table. The court assembled, the booze flowed, the chatter seemed endless. After our first night together in Frank's suite, I was in constant attendance at his table. Frank wanted it that way. I loved it that way.

I never assumed that I was the only woman in his life, and I never presumed any exclusive rights to possession. I also understood that career demands on his time had to be met. I knew that, while not so structured as the business environment I had known in New York, the entertainment business also had its conferences, negotiations, rehearsals, private as well as public imperatives.

Whatever Frank wanted for Frank would come in due course. With the first magnitude of stardom he had achieved came comfortable perks. Responsibility was part of the price. Frank always paid the price. I accepted him and his realities as they both were. He had already completed the films "Suddenly," "Young At Heart," "Not As A Stranger," "The Tender Trap," "Guys And Dolls," and "From Here To Eternity," before we met. He was recognized and appreciated as a talented actor, but loved by millions of adoring fans, and me, as a magnificent singer and performer on stage.

When at Frank's table, I sat either next to him or directly across from him. The entourage took their cue from him in their attitudes towards me, ladies included. Throughout our romance and the many years of friendship that followed, Frank treated me as a lady whose values and social tastes were to be respected. The celebrants at his table always did the same, with perhaps just a touch of deference.

As a respite from the sorrows and cares I was addressing, being with Frank was more than ideal. Mostly, with Frank, it was fun, without the pressures of emotional strains.

I recall only one incident when a little conflict imposed on the tranquility we shared. Lauren Bacall and Humphrey Bogart were among Frank's intimate friends. They had a standing invitation to his table when in Las Vegas. One evening, Lauren appeared alone.

The early years of Lauren's and my background included some similarities. We were both reared in Brooklyn and we both had successful modeling careers. But in personality and tastes, we were very different, except for our mutual interest in Frank Sinatra. Lauren had gravitated to Hollywood to seek a career as an actress and she did some very good work. Previously, I had no interest in a career, other than to be a wife, mother and homemaker. My divorce and meeting Frank had changed all that.

Lauren appeared this particular evening dressed in jeans and shirt, the accepted chic garb of the movie set in the fifties. My dress was equally casual, but by New York standards. Both she and New York would loosen up about dress — but in a distant day. Even then, I never affected the studiedly casual jeans-and-shirt leisure wear.

Maybe it's too much of a challenge to my inherent tastes. To this day, I try to dress with simple elegance, formal or informal. I was, I like to remember, elegant, but informally dressed in a custom-tailored white linen, street-length dress, appliqued in a tasteful white-on-white design from the left shoulder to the bottom hem. I was comfortable. Frank had told me that I "looked terrific" in that dress, that he liked seeing me in it.

Maybe his approval was the problem, but Lauren let me know, quite loudly, in the presence of all at the table, that I was overdressed. It wasn't a friendly woman-to-woman comment. I remember it as a very sarcastic, snide remark.

With the discernment I would learn to respect about Frank, he quietly whispered in my ear; "Don't pay any attention to that."

Throughout our romance and friendship, Frank disclosed a remarkable sensitivity and high degree of propriety. Perhaps he reflected the ethic of a day when men were expected to treat a woman as a lady until she proved otherwise and even then was to be given some consideration. He was always kind and generous to the waiters, waitresses, busboys, parking valets, anyone who served him. I could tell he truly cared for those less fortunate. Whatever the reasons, that relationship is an appreciated memory.

Frank was making plenty of money. His world was tailored clothes, haute cuisine, fine liquors and champagnes, and plenty of all. A lavish suite was provided him on his tours. He deserved the best. Sometimes he demanded it. He always got it. Wherever he went, his reception was more than "top drawer," it was royal. Frank never lost sight of his humble beginnings. He was well aware of the abilities he was blessed with and he worked very hard to refine and perfect his talents. He always gives his very best to his audiences. Frank also has given much more. He always gave lavish tips to waiters, waitresses, the maitre d's and others who served him. His trademark tip then was a $100 bill. Yet he always maintained a sense of decorum in my presence and towards me. Yes, there were gifts, but nothing elaborate. At no time did he misuse money to taint our sharing.

But we had shared more than we knew, and a dark cloud would soon cast its pall over my life.

CHAPTER II

It was December 15, 1955 and my thoughts were on my daughters, Kathy and Diane. We had never been apart for any length of time, and never for Christmas. I telephoned my husband's lawyer in New York and told him I wanted the children to be with me in Las Vegas for the holidays. He said he would speak to my husband and arrange it. He did.

I greeted them at McCarran Field on December 20, and a joyous reunion it was. The next day we went shopping for a Christmas tree and all the trimmings. The girls spotted one which had been sprayed pink. They had to have it. We spent the evening trimming the tree and talking and talking and talking. This would our first Christmas without their father. We had a grand time as we trimmed the tree and had popcorn and sodas.

During the next week I was totally devoted to my girls. Frank understood and would join us when he could. He loved watching them and their girlish giggles and excitement over all their holiday spirits. I took them to Lake Mead, Hoover Dam and other sights close by. They really enjoyed Las Vegas, especially the weather. Christmas morning was wonderful. I had purchased everything on their wish lists. Frank had sent gifts, too, giant stuffed animals for Kathy and Diane which he had picked out himself in the gift shop in the Sands. He also had sent a beaded red evening bag for me. I loved it.

As good times will be, it was over all too soon. At the airport, my daughters and I hugged our love and kissed our goodbyes, wiping each others' tears away. Their departure was a sight which touched my soul, it was both comical and heart-rending. I watched as they trudged up the moveable stairway to the aircraft clutching those big stuffed animals to their hearts. I watched through my tears as the airplane lifted into the clear blue heaven, wondering when I would have them with me again.

New Year's Eve in Las Vegas was like no other place in the world. It was one giant party in all the hotels and casinos, with people spilling out onto the streets. Everyone was in a happy, party mood. Frank and I spent one of the happiest New Year's celebrations of my life, together. After his shows, we joined the ever-present crowd in the Sands and enjoyed a tremendous feast. We toasted the new year, wishing good health and all good things to everyone.

I had been in Las Vegas since November 10, 1955. My divorce would be granted on January 12, 1956. Legally, I could then return to New York. But Frank was still appearing at the Sands and I didn't want to leave him. I also did not want to return to the cold and snow of New York. My daughters were in boarding school, so there was really nothing to force me back to New York.

Frank asked me to accompany him to Los Angeles for a couple of days while he had a business meeting there. I welcomed the invitation, especially because I had never been to Los Angeles before.

We took the one A.M. train from Las Vegas to Union Station in downtown Los Angeles. It was a relaxed, fun way to travel and allowed us some extra private time. I remember one of Frank's musing comments to me on the train. "You remind me of my wife," he said. I've often wondered if he meant Ava. An observer might consider if he meant Nancy. He never said, and I didn't ask. His meaning remains an enigma.

Frank had a home off Coldwater Canyon, up from the Beverly Hills Hotel. It was a rambling ranch house, tastefully furnished with a private road leading to its gated entrance. His staff had everything prepared for our arrival and they were particularly nice and friendly to me. I could see they adored Frank, and he must have treated them very well.

We spent two days at his home and it was wonderful. He had to go to a couple of meetings in town, but he would return home and we would be together. Dinner was prepared by his cook and served by his manservant, George Jacobs.

Los Angeles in the midfifties was a refreshing change from New York. The metropolitan area sprawled south and west of the Santa Monica and San Gabriel Mountains, building out, rather than up.

In winter, the San Gabriels lifted snow-capped peaks into the breath-takingly clear sky, inspiring humble awareness of both beauty man has not matched and the ageless power of God and all his nature.

Sunshine bathed the area, its rays as yet not so filtered by the smog which years later would cast its pall along the mountain shield and creep across the city to dim its splendor.

"Beautiful People" (as they liked to be called) lazed and tanned while wet-suited surfers played in the breakers rolling to the shore. I fell in love with Los Angeles.

The return trip to Las Vegas was pleasant. I felt glad to be back and we resumed our routine. Destiny would bring me back to Los Angeles soon, without Frank, on a most unpleasant mission.

Shortly after our train trip, when we had arrived back in Las Vegas, I found myself pregnant. I am a one-man woman, and there could be no doubt who the father was. I decided not to tell Frank. I did confide in Eleanor and Beverly, Carmen Dell and Sonny Small. Carmen and Sonny were in the chorus line at the El Rancho Hotel. Carmen was a neighbor at the Sans Souci Apartments where I lived and a trusted friend. She knew of a doctor in Los Angeles who would perform the necessary operation for $500.

An abortion! I was again thrust into mental turmoil. Abortions were not common in the United States then and were considered to be a very risky procedure, as well as illegal. Time was critical. I was torn between the desire to have the child and knowing that marriage between Frank and myself would never work.

My heart was aching, and I was scared. I wanted to have the baby but there were so many, many things against this decision. There were so many other people to be concerned about.

What would this do to Frank? His career? What would he say? My worst fears: Would he hate me? Would he lose respect for me? I knew in my heart he would not abandon me, that he would insist on doing the right thing. I was terrified that this rectitude would destroy any feelings he may have for me. I was also concerned about Kathy and Diane.

I made the agonizing decision to have the operation. Carmen insisted on flying to Los Angeles with me. We took a cab to the doctor's office which was on Wilshire Boulevard near La Brea. The reception room was well appointed and tasteful, with soothing colors, soft lighting and lush plants. The examination room, where the operation would be performed, had an obvious antiseptic smell. At least I felt I was in capable hands. Sodium Pentothal was administered and the procedure completed without complications.

When I awakened, the doctor remarked: "Miss Graham, you are quite a woman." I often wonder what I may have said under the influence of the drug. Did I tell him Frank Sinatra was the father? What did I say?

Carmen and I stayed in Los Angeles for the night and returned to Las Vegas the following morning. The next day I had some discomfort, but the prescription the doctor had given me worked wonders. I kept to myself for a while, telling Frank and friends that I was fighting the flu.

As I had requested, Eleanor, Beverly, Carmen and Sonny never said a word to Frank, or anyone. Who says a woman can't keep a secret? Their silence was a perfect exhibit of true friendship. I value my closeness with each of them to this day, although time and distance has separated us.

I like to feel that I have always been able to control my emotions. My heart rules my head, but my mind controls my body. I tell of this part of my life for the first time publicly. I chose to have the abortion without consulting Frank because I did not want to hold up a man for a mistake where I was equally responsible. I believe that each such situation has its own set of circumstances and the woman must make what, to me, was an agonizing decision. If I had borne a child with Frank, out of wedlock, the tabloid press would have pounced on him. I did not want to be the cause of unhappiness to Frank. The result would not only have affected our lives, but also both our families as well.

Back in Las Vegas, and with Frank, I was faced with another decision. Now that my divorce was final, the operation over, what would I do now? I was financially secure, but I did not want to return to New York. Although I loved Las Vegas and enjoyed being there with Frank, I did not feel Las Vegas was the right place for me at the time.

I decided on Los Angeles. I flew back to New York to make plans for the big move. I had to close the apartment, sell the furniture and fixtures, and make certain of the arrangements for both Kathy and Diane's boarding school and relocating them with me once I was settled in Los Angeles. There were so many things to do.

In New York, I enthused about Los Angeles to my good friend, Rita Canzoneri. Rita was recently divorced from Tony Canzoneri, twice world lightweight boxing champion. She caught my fervor, and we made plans to relocate to Los Angeles together. Within a few weeks, I had completed my chores in New York, and we were ready for the move. We decided to fly to Las Vegas first so I could say farewell to all my friends there and Rita could meet Frank.

At dinner with Frank, he pointed out a small detail about my living in Los Angeles which had completely escaped me. I did not have a car. Unlike Manhattan, you can exist in Los Angeles without one, but you can't live in Los Angeles without one, Frank said. I wanted a 1956 Ford Thunderbird, which later became a classic. I quickly found they were in short supply. I had been told by a friend who was knowledgeable about buying cars that I could possibly get a demonstrator with very low miles for a price of around $3,000. New, the T-Birds were going for nearly $4,000. I visited both Ford dealers in Las Vegas. Neither had a Thunderbird demonstrator for immediate sale, and they told me it would take six to eight weeks to order one. Getting a demonstrator would take even longer. Also, as is a woman's prerogative, I specifically wanted an all-white one.

I told Frank about my car problem. He asked how much I intended to spend on a car. I told him $3,000 was all I could afford at the time, and that I was told I should look for a T-Bird demonstrator. Frank said he would speak to some friends to see what he could do.

About a two weeks later, Frank called me and asked me to join him for lunch at the Sands. After lunch, Frank took me to the rear entrance of the hotel. There it sat: a 1956 Thunderbird, white, with red interior and red wheel rims. I was astonished! How did he do it, and so fast? I learned later he had the dealer paint it white for me. He had gotten it from a New Jersey dealer who had it shipped to Las Vegas. I was thrilled. This car, a little two-seater promoted as the first American sports car, had style. Frank told me the total cost was $3,000. I gave him a check. Later, the more I thought about it, the more I knew it must have cost more, especially with the cost of shipping it from New Jersey and all. Frank had lied to me, but, oh what a wonderful lie.

Rita and I spent another week in Las Vegas. We had several reasons: to relax, for me to have time to adjust to my new T-Bird, and for me to be with Frank until his singing engagement ended.

Then June 10, 1956 arrived: It was time to make the Los Angeles move official. Rita and I said our farewells, jumped into the shiny new T-Bird and headed for Los Angeles. Optimistic and young at heart, we were both off to start our lives anew. We decided to share the driving and make the trip nonstop, about a six-hour drive. Rita was driving and we pulled off the highway to get gas and change drivers.

As we left the highway and approached an intersection, Rita was still moving practically at highway speed. The car in front had already stopped. I can still hear the squeal of the tires, smell the burning rubber, see my life flashing through my mind, and watch Rita's face turning as white as her knuckles as she gripped the steering wheel. She was practically rising out of her seat as she stood on the brakes.

The squeal of the tires stopped and we felt a slight bump as the nose of the T-Bird gently kissed the rear of the big Buick in front of us. I quickly climbed over Rita into the driver's seat. Rita had no valid license. I exited the car and met the Buick's driver in the middle. We were both amazed that neither car had a scratch. I was so relieved as I said my silent thanks to God.

The old man driving the Buick asked if I or my passenger were hurt. My answer, of course, was no. He smiled and said, "Have a nice day." I got back in the car. Rita and I just looked at each other and started to laugh. I decided to drive my own precious little car the rest of the way to what was often called the Pink Palace, the Beverly Hills Hotel.

After checking in we bought a Sunday edition of the Los Angeles Times. We spent Sunday afternoon driving around the city seeking a suitable lodging. After many disappointments, we located a lovely two-bedroom, two-bath apartment on the ground floor of the Fountain Lanai

Apartments, a nice two-story building on the then-fashionable stretch of Fountain Avenue in West Hollywood. We then set out to familiarize ourselves with The City of Angels. Life in Los Angeles would prove far more exciting than I suspected.

Frank had two homes in California. The one off Coldwater Canyon in Los Angeles and the other in Palm Springs. Both his homes were modest, considering his income. Frank did not seem to need the ostentatious splendor affected by many of lesser status than he had earned. His homes were comfortable, nicely furnished, and cozy. The seclusion of the Palm Springs home on the Tamarisk Country Club Golf Course would later fall victim to fame for reasons other than the fact it was his. Frank had it enlarged several times to accommodate President John F. Kennedy, along with JFK's aides, advisors, confidants and, of course, his Secret Service agents.

Rita would come along at times when I went to visit Frank in town, and he welcomed her as a trusted friend. Remember, privacy around Frank Sinatra usually included one of his closest friends, Jilly Rizzo, along with Hank Sanicola, Jimmy Van Heusen, and more. Gatherings around him were always exciting and different. No one could ever claim boredom. But my life was about to be energized in a way I would dread.

Chapter III

s I settled into Los Angeles, I drifted for the first few months. Disorientation is not unusual in any change of environment, and the adjustment to Los Angeles after New York and Las Vegas was an epic cultural shift from the concrete canyons of New York and the desert playground. At times I would not see Frank for months on end, but I was always surprised and pleased when he called. It was a lift from my self-imposed quiet existence, in which I spent a lot of time at home with my hobbies. From my days as a showroom model in New York, where designers would fit their creations on me, I had learned their intricate techniques and was able to fashion my own wardrobe. I also enjoyed oil painting and sculpting in clay. My new apartment in Los Angeles inspired me to devote more time to these relaxing endeavors. My alimony was $2,000 per month, which in 1956 was more than ample, so finding work was not imperative.

Because we were in Hollywood, many people were urging me to try for a career in films. "Why not?" I thought, so I joined the Screen Actors Guild. I had a new composite photo portfolio made and arranged appointments with various agents. Soon, I had walk-on roles in a couple of "B" movies. However, I knew inside of me that I had no aspirations of becoming an actress. My focus remained on settling down and bringing my daughters from New York, we missed each other so.

My social life was as busy as I wanted it to be, especially because I was a new single woman in town. I often would join friends at the Polo Lounge at the Beverly Hills Hotel. In those days the lounge was always fascinating, you never knew what celebrity would be sitting at the next table. Dino, the famous maitre d' of the Polo Lounge, kept vigil and protected us from being bothered by anyone he didn't know to be a gentleman. Dino was a master of his position; he remembered everyone by name. I did accept various dinner and party invitations with gentlemen I had met through friends. Slowly, I was gathering a nice circle of acquaintances.

Rita was doing quite well with her own pursuits. She had met a charming young writer named David Chandler. They became constant companions and eventually married. Rita became an actor's agent and made quite a name for herself in the industry.

Being new in town, I asked friends to refer me to a good doctor and a dentist I could rely on for my children and myself. I made an appointment with a doctor for a physical. All sorts of tests were taken. My blood pressure was fine, my heart was fine, I was in good physical condition. A routine PAP smear was taken. The doctor told me he would have the results of all the tests within a week.

A few days later, the doctor telephoned me. I said a bright, cheery "Good morning." His words were chilling.

"Miss Graham, you are in general good health, your EKG, your blood work are all fine, but the lab found an indication of cancer of the uterus," he said coldly, without a trace of emotion or compassion. Instead of asking me to come into his office, he was delivering this terrible news to me over the telephone. "So much for bedside manners," I later thought.

"CANCER!" I shrieked. That was impossible, I thought to myself. I felt a cold sweat popping out all over my body. I began to feel dizzy, as though I were going to faint. I tried to compose myself, sitting in silence for a few minutes, though it seemed like hours. The doctor spoke again:

"We have to get you in here immediately. You need a hysterectomy!"

I hung up the telephone and sat in my chair, trembling.

Cancer even now is a word associated with terror. In 1957, it was more so. I was feeling all that terror and more. The descriptions of its arduous treatment, attrition of the body and spirit, agonizing pain and, too frequently, a slow death, had been graphically publicized all over the country. The prospect of being a victim of this dreaded disease was too much to be accepted objectively. Today, publicity encouraging preventive measures, new early detection methods and advances in medical science in treating cancer have greatly improved survival chances, a fact also true of cancer of the uterus. Not only has the incidence of the scourge dropped to one-third its 1950s level, but the death rate has been reduced to a very small percentage of those afflicted.

But I heard those words in 1957, when the disease was fatal far more frequently. Thoughts and panic were rushing through my mind. I was just starting a new life. I didn't want to die. Who would raise the children? I had to think, calmly and logically, about what to do. I knew few people well enough in California to reach out to. I didn't want to scare my family back East. I began to pray. I prayed that I could be provided the physical strength and the mental courage to beat this monstrous killer. I have always held firmly a belief in God within me.

I thought of Frank. I called and spoke to his secretary Gloria Lovell, and informed her of what my doctor had said.

"I'll get back to you as soon as I find out from Mr. Sinatra what to do," she replied.

It was a day or two before I heard back from her. Frank made arrangements for me to be admitted to the City of Hope, a renowned cancer research center in Duarte, California. He had connections. Going through regular channels, the City of Hope Hospital had a waiting list of up to two or three years. Gloria told me who to see at the time of my admission. I was admitted within days of Gloria's call. For the following five days, a series of tests was done and a conization performed.

A conization is a procedure where the doctors take a cone-shaped sample from the uterus, slice it in thin slivers and perform biopsies to determine how far the cancer has progressed and what treatment is required for best possible results of recovery. At the end of the five days, I was released to go home and await the results of the tests. More waiting. Agonizing waiting.

All during the time I was in the hospital and while at home awaiting the results, I prayed and prayed. Waiting for anything of importance can be taxing, but this was an ordeal. My anxiety was hard to bear.

It took nearly three weeks before I heard from the nurse who had been caring for me. I was simply told to return to the hospital to see the doctor; she could not tell me anything about the tests results. This certainly was not what I was waiting to hear, and panicky thoughts were creeping in. I drove alone to Duarte, fear gnawing in my gut.

When I arrived the chief oncologist and gynecologist sat down in his office and looked at me. He had a big smile on his face.

"Miss Graham, I'm very pleased to tell you this. Our tests show no sign of cancer ... not in any of the biopsies and examinations," he said.

I was speechless. The doctors were all certain of the cancer in the PAP smear. The chief oncologist could only surmise that since the first diagnosis and my hospitalization, my own defense system had beaten the illness in its incipient stage. Personally, I like to believe the cancer retreated because of my prayers, my inner strength and Frank Sinatra in my corner.

However, the specter would still cloud my days for a long time. Testing was required in three weeks, then every three months, then every six months. Meanwhile, I had my files transferred to a Dr. Leon "Red" Krohn, Frank's friend, one of the finest gynecologists in Beverly Hills, who watched me closely for several years.

I regained my strength and felt I had been given a reprieve. I began searching for a good private boarding school for Kathy and Diane and decided on the Anokia School in Arcadia, about an hour's drive from Los Angeles. With the girls in school, I could work during the week and have them home with me on weekends. When I told them, they were ecstatic. They could not wait to see Disneyland, me and Los Angeles, in that order — Disneyland indeed was their first priority.

Arrangements were made to bring them out in late August so I could enroll them in school. I was anxiously awaiting their arrival. As the plane landed, my heart throbbed. When they caught sight of me waving, they ran to my open arms, and I gave them an enormous hug. We spent the entire weekend just hugging, talking, hugging and talking and enjoying ourselves together again ... at last. The following week we drove to Disneyland where we spent four fun-filled days. It was such a joy watching them in this wonderland, but I paid the price. My feet ached for two weeks after.

Then, in the succeeding two weeks before they entered school, we toured Los Angeles, seeing all the pretty and famous sights. We went to museums, the La Brea Tar Pits, the zoo, a drive into the mountains for a picnic and, of course, movies. We were so close and I felt good having them with me again.

Then we plunged into the serious side of life. We went shopping for school supplies, and personal items, undergarments, nightclothes and robes, all of which had to have their names sewn in. At school they wore uniforms which had to be purchased through the school. I brought them to Anokia School for a tour, and they were introduced to the principal, their teachers and their houseparent. They now were excited and anxious to go there.

With the girls comfortably settled at Anokia, I continued to do occasional walk-ons in various television and motion picture films. I looked forward to the end of the day at the Polo Lounge, where I would join my friends for happy hour.

I could always depend on an amiable crowd and an atmosphere where everyone could unwind and let their hair down. This is where I met Sy DeVore, who would soon play an important role in my future. Sy was of medium height, trim, in his midforties. He had an appearance of a self-made man and a personality that was gregarious and appealing. We soon developed a warm, platonic friendship.

The month of September passed into October with signs of fall appearing in the trees and air. I was content with my life in Los Angeles.

Sy DeVore was noted as "The Haberdasher To The Stars." Sy had built a very successful business catering to gentlemen in the film industry, actors and studio executives alike. His was an easily identifiable look which marked the wearer as a discerning man of taste, Hollywood style. Sy's shop was on Vine Street near the famous Brown Derby restaurant where celebrities came to hold their power lunches, to see and be seen. It was also close to NBC Television studios, Paramount studios and others.

Sy's birthday fell on Halloween. That gave him two good reasons to host a lavish party, which he did every year. His parties were legendary in Hollywood, always something special. Traditionally, this party was one of Sy's best. It was well-recognized as a fun costume party of the year, even by Hollywood standards. In time, among the rising stars, producers, directors, anybody who was or soon to be anybody, might show up at Sy's. Sy invited me to his birthday/Halloween party of 1957.

I have been told that my almond eyes and high cheek bones looked very Oriental. How else should I go, then, but as a Japanese "geisha girl?" I purchased several yards of silk material, then designed and made my own costume. I like to remember the authentic look of my eye-catching bright pink kimono set off by a broad gold obi.

Patty Lloyd, a friend and neighbor, shared a cab to the party with me. We arrived at around eight-thirty P.M., and the party was in full swing. I had never been to a Hollywood bash, and I was awestruck at the number of people crowded into his expansive, lovely home at the foot of Beverly Hills. A butler opened the door and escorted us into the foyer, where Sy greeted us. Leading us through the crowd, making introductions along the way, he took us to the long buffet piled high with a dazzling array of food. White-gloved waiters stood poised to serve up our selections and take our drink orders. Sy disappeared and I chose a small plate of jumbo shrimp and a portion of lobster salad. A waiter brought me a vodka sour.

I spotted an empty Queen Anne chair by the fireplace in the formal living room and sat down to eat and watch the crowd. I noticed that Sy made a point of rushing to the door to welcome new arrivals personally. He would then wind them through the crowd to the buffet, introducing them along the way as he had done with us. He was such a gracious host. The large living room, foyer, formal dining room and patio were decorated for Halloween and a brightly colored banner stretched across the massive patio entryway extolling: "Happy Birthday and Happy Halloween, too."

Aside from Sy, Patty and a few of the Polo Lounge crowd, everyone else was a stranger to me. To compound the problem, recognizing anyone was difficult because we were all in costume, strange makeup and masks. Many of those costumes were borrowed from the wardrobe departments of the movie studios or rented from Western Costume Co. The crowd was constantly changing, people coming and going. I spoke with several of the people I knew from the Polo Lounge. I accepted compliments on the originality of my costume with modesty and graciously commented on theirs.

Around ten P.M., the butler opened the door and in stepped the most handsome man I had ever seen. He was not in costume, but instead a meticulously tailored dark business suit, white shirt, burgundy silk tie and pocket handkerchief clad his six-foot-two frame. He was the proverbial tall, dark and handsome man. Sy was right there and greeted him warmly, then began leading him to the buffet and bar, in the opposite direction from where I was seated. From a distance of about twenty feet, he looked over his shoulder. As our eyes met, he smiled, and I returned his smile. Then the two men disappeared into the crowd.

A few minutes later, I caught sight of him again as he was making his way through the maze of people, sans Sy. He was looking right at me, and caught me staring at him. I felt myself blush as I vainly tried to turn my eyes away. He stopped a waiter and said something to him, then he proceeded to walk toward me.

As he approached, the waiter appeared with a tray of fresh drinks. He took two and came directly to me.

Handing me a drink, he said:

"A fresh vodka sour for the pretty lady in pink?"

"Thank you, that was very thoughtful of you," I replied.

"My name is Richard Diamond ... and yours?" he asked.

"How do you do? I'm Ellie Graham," I responded, shaking his hand.

"Quite a party, isn't it?" he said, looking amused.

"It's lovely, very entertaining," I replied.

"You're from the East, aren't you?" he quizzed, with a degree of certainty in his voice.

"Yes, New York, but I live here now."

"What do you do here?"

"I paint, sculpt and design and make my own clothes."

"That's very interesting ..., but, what do you do for work?"

"I'm not employed steadily, as yet. I just relocated and have my girls in boarding school in Arcadia, so I'm still getting settled in,"

"And is there a Mister Graham?"

"Uh ... no ... I was divorced last year," I responded, thinking to myself, "Here is this gorgeous guy, whom I know nothing about, yet I am answering all these probing questions without hesitation. Am I scaring him away?" Yet I could not resist talking to him. He had a very sexy voice.

His smile was warm, friendly; his sparkling brown eyes seemed to be looking deep inside me. His California tan complemented his dark brown wavy hair. I was not prepared for his magnetic charm and the chemistry that seemed to be pulling us together. I decided to turn the tables:

"What type of business are you in?" I asked, thinking to myself he must be a big movie star whose screen presence had thus far escaped me because I was not a movie buff.

"I'm a private detective," he answered, unassumingly.

"Oh, that must be very interesting work, especially in Hollywood," I said, not wanting to appear as though I were prying.

"Yes it is," he said, flashing his broad smile.

"You mentioned girls, how many children do you have?"

"Two."

Now I was getting a little nervous. Here I am at a lavish Hollywood party, revealing much information to this total stranger who is a private detective. He seemed to be extracting my entire life story in ten minutes of conversation. What if he were hired by my former husband to get some dirt on me, to try and take my girls away? I decided to evade any further personal questions, at least until I knew more about him.

Just then Sy appeared, put his arm around my shoulder and said:

"David, I see you have met my lovely friend, Ellie, one of our town's most eligible ladies."

"Yes, we were just getting acquainted," the mysterious stranger said, with a sly smile.

"Ellie, David Janssen is one of our most eligible bachelors, and one of my best customers too," Sy said.

"I must be confused ... I thought your name is Richard," I blurted out.

"Oh, it is, on television. He's 'Richard Diamond — Private Eye.' He has his own TV series," Sy exclaimed, breaking into a loud, roaring laugh, acknowledging David's clever wit.

It was my first insight into David's wry and unique sense of humor.

"I take it you're not a fan. You don't watch television?"

"I'm sorry, I very seldom watch TV. News, mostly, or an occasional variety show or special," I answered, sounding almost apologetic.

"I'd like you to watch mine sometime. It's on Saturday nights at ten, on NBC. I'd really like your opinion," he said, sounding very sincere.

"I will make it a point to."

I observed the way he lit my cigarette, then his. The way he would stand straight when others approached us. He was so debonair, so charming, such a gentleman. Knowing that he was not really a private detective and not married, I was able to relax and began to watch him more closely. By this time, we were on our third round of drinks together. I am not a drinker, so I was sipping my drink very slowly.

I noted how so many people would intrude on our conversation, just to be certain to say hello to him. It was obvious that he was well known in the television industry. I was much impressed.

David did not leave my side throughout the evening. We were both amused at the variety of costumes and how people would go to such great lengths to make themselves look foolish. As midnight approached the crowd was very festive, and the trio was playing "Satin Doll." He motioned toward the music, took my hand and we weaved our way, hand in hand to the small area allotted for dancing.

He held me close, being careful not to step on my toes. He had his own beat, which was not necessarily that of the music. Even so, it felt good in his arms. I was hoping he would ask for my phone number.

David asked if I was with anyone at the party. I told him that I had come with a friend who had left moments before he arrived. It seemed strange he would ask that, because I had been with him for the past two hours. He then asked if he could escort me home.

"Was he reading my mind?" I wondered. I told him I was prepared to take a taxi, but he would not hear of that. "Thank God," I thought to myself. We stayed for about another hour, maybe longer. I was quite tired and I sensed he was, too.

We began searching for Sy to express our birthday wishes and to again express our gratitude for a lovely party. David spotted a friend from his studio, a man who apparently had quite a bit to drink and David asked if I would object to giving the man a ride to his West Hollywood apartment. Of course, I had no objections.

I was surprised when the parking valet brought David's car. It was a black 1957 T-Bird. The drive was rather snug, with the three of us in the two-seater and me squeezed in the middle. On the way to his friend's apartment, David suggested we stop at an all-night diner for coffee. Again, no objections from me. David wanted to sober up his friend, at least a little. And I was looking forward to his opening up to me.

CHAPTER IV

It was nearly three A.M. when we arrived at my apartment, which was a short distance from his friend's. I could see David was very, very tired. He escorted me to my door. I took his hand to thank him, then said:

"Would you like to come in and have one for the road ... coffee, I mean?"

"I thought you'd never ask. I have a long drive to the valley."

I put on a fresh pot of Maxwell House. I could hear David turn on the hi-fi. I came into the living room with our coffee on a tray. He had removed his jacket, laid it carefully over a chair and loosened his tie. He was seated on the sofa. It was Saturday, November 1, 1957.

We sat on the sofa having our coffee and talked and talked and talked. He remarked how beautiful he found me. How flattering. He smiled when I complimented him on his manners. We talked about my marriage, why it ended. He wanted to know all about Kathy and Diane and how the divorce affected them. He was somewhat surprised when I mentioned that I was dating Frank. He changed the subject quickly, and I was glad he did. All that seemed to matter to him was that we were together, and I felt that way too.

He began opening up about himself. He told me he had never been married, he was 28 years old, born in Napanee, Nebraska. He described his mother Berniece, who had been a Ziegfeld Follies girl and toured with the group. He had wanted to be a runner, make it to the Olympics and become a professional, but a high school knee injury had ended those dreams. His mother had then mapped his career in motion pictures. He had served in the Army during the Korean conflict, but he was stationed in California making training films for the troops. He had completed his actor's training at Universal Studios and appeared in several of their "forgettable films," as he laughingly referred to them.

He then went into a graphic description of his starring role as "Richard Diamond — Private Eye." The series had been on NBC Television Network for over a year. It was his first major, steady acting role. He felt deep and abiding respect for Dick Powell, the producer of the series, and his lovely wife, June Allyson, herself a major star in feature films and television. David was confident that his forté would be in television as opposed to feature films. Dick Powell had convinced him that television was the wave of the future. Doing a TV series was far more demanding on an actor than working in feature films. David was modest, but he showed an inner feeling that he was comfortable in his hopes for the future.

David spoke glowingly of his stepfather Gene Janssen. David had taken his name and considered him his real father. He adored his two half sisters, Teri and Jill, both still in school.

As we sat on the sofa, the dawn light began filtering in through the living room windows. I suggested it would be better if he stayed and slept on the couch for a few hours. He readily accepted. I closed the drapes and got him some bedding from the hall linen closet. We said our goodnights-goodmornings and I retired to my bedroom.

I awakened at ten-thirty A.M. and peeked out my bedroom door. He was still sleeping. I hurried to shower and put on my makeup before he could catch sight of me without it.

I slipped past him into the kitchen. I made a fresh pot of coffee and was preparing freshly squeezed orange juice, when David awoke at the sound of the juicer. I took coffee and juice out to him and offered to prepare breakfast, but he suggested we have brunch at the Beverly Hills Hotel. He freshened up and we left for the hotel. As we drove back to my apartment afterward, he asked me to join him for dinner that evening. I had to decline because I had accepted a dinner invitation from Frank, although I didn't tell David that. He asked if I would be free for dinner Sunday, and I accepted.

Later that afternoon I was on the telephone when the doorbell rang. It was a delivery of two dozen red roses. They were from David. What a delifghtful surprise. That evening, during dinner, I told Frank about Sy's party and about meeting David Janssen. He said he knew who he was but didn't know him.

Frank didn't think David was much of a star and really didn't seem to care. Even so, all during dinner my thoughts were on David and seeing him again on Sunday. Frank must have sensed something. Shortly after dinner, he suggested we make it an early evening and he drove me home. He kissed me goodnight and told me he would call me later.

Unlike my liaison with Frank, my feelings for David were immediate, strong, real. I was feeling love for the first time in my life. I had a difficult time sleeping that night. Sunday I drove to Arcadia and took the girls to lunch and a movie. I arrived back home at around five o'clock. I wanted to be prepared when David called for me. I took a leisurely bubble bath, freshened my manicure and fixed my hair. Then, the big decision: What to wear? I took more than two hours to get ready.

David was prompt. He had chosen a small family-owned French bistro off Sunset Boulevard. It was not a touristy place, instead having very cozy romantic lighting and soft French music piped in. We were warmly greeted and I could tell it was one of David's favorite haunts. I remember that the food was marvelous, as he had promised, and the red table wine was exceptional. Everything about the dinner was perfect.

We sat and talked about everything. I was truly surprised to discover that David was a real intellectual. His interests covered so many subjects; world history, current world events, art, just about everything. I also learned that he was an avid reader and that he read an average of two to three books a week. I was so interested in learning all I could about him, I remained silent except when I had to encourage him to continue talking.

David was a little shy and reserved when he first met people, but if he liked someone, he would open up and his charming personality and quick wit would mesmerize all around him. I was captivated listening to his dissertations about so many interesting subjects.

After our demitasse, we returned to my apartment. I asked him to come in for a nightcap. As I prepared his Scotch and soda and a vodka sour for myself, I could hear him putting albums on the hi-fi. We sat on the sofa continuing where we left off. He was so easy to be with, so down-to-earth. I later would learn that he was also a workaholic. He had a definite plan for his career and felt the "Diamond" series would be his stepping stone to greater and more prominent roles. He believed in Dick Powell and was concentrating on television instead of the feature film roles being offered him.

We laughed easily together. His sense of humor was well honed, and he could joke about anything, but mostly he would poke fun at himself. He revealed to me that he was a homebody, that he loved his work, but preferred to go home and not be so public. There were many publicity events and personal appearances the studio required of him, but he took it as part of the job.

After swearing me to Girl Scouts' honor, he divulged his secret of having to fortify himself with a few Scotch and sodas before making the required public appearances. After they were completed, he would retreat to his little castle and be his real self. He lamented that being in the TV world, he was often recognized and always felt self-conscious of his appearance, his dress, his manners.

I would soon learn that he was an intense man who had an innate gene which would cause him to go to excesses in many areas, not all of which would be healthy. The lesson, for as long as I was with him, was striking, strong and bittersweet.

The clock struck midnight and he told me he had an early call at the studio. I wanted so much for him to stay, but I said nothing. I walked him to the door, he paused, then held me gently in his arms and gave me a warm, loving kiss. Then he asked if I would have dinner with him again the next evening. I was thrilled.

Over the course of the next several weeks, we became inseparable. David took me to a different restaurant every night. Nothing fancy, just quiet intimate places for young lovers. And, like Cinderella, my prince each night would kiss me goodnight, then vanish into the night.

I felt like a high school girl with her first true love. Over the past weeks, we had really become close. I had been completely open and honest with David. I held practically nothing back from him. Any questions he asked about me, I answered truthfully. I am certain that he was honest with me and the more I learned about him, the deeper my love for him grew.

We had visited Kathy and Diane on weekends and taken them to Disneyland and other fun places. He seemed to have much pleasure with them, and they adored him. He would tease them in a way that would have them giggling, and we would join in their laughter. I was pleased and relieved to see how they all got along so well. Good thing, because they were to see much more of each other.

Saturday was a typically beautiful southern California day when I went to visit the girls at Anokia. I was in a wonderful mood, though I could only take them out for the afternoon. I was to meet David at five-thirty P.M. He had invited me to dinner at his cottage, where he was cooking the one meal he knew how to make without mishaps.

When I arrived he had nuts and miniature pretzels on the wet bar which flanked the left side of the homey living room. A comfortable overstuffed sofa and two easy chairs were placed opposite the fireplace. The kitchen was about four or five steps up from the living room and, as I was soon to find out, the bedroom was off the next landing.

He greeted me with a big kiss, a kitchen towel tucked into his trousers and an anxious look on his face. I know he wanted everything to be perfect so I would be favorably impressed.

"Can I get you a drink?" he asked.

A bottle of Mr. & Mrs. T's was on the bar, so I knew a Bloody Mary was what he had in mind for me. He knew that vodka was the only alcoholic beverage I could handle.

"A Bloody Mary would be just fine," I replied.

"How was your visit with the kids?" he inquired.

I told him of the afternoon's events as he fixed the drinks. We sat at the bar and nibbled as we had our drinks, then moved to the sofa. The fireplace was crackling, even though it was a little early in the season to have the fireplace going. Despite that fact, the fire created the warm and romantic mood which was to follow.

Dinner wasn't cooked until well past eleven o'clock. Thanks to the soft music, dim lights and intoxicating drinks, we were in his bedroom within an hour of my arrival. He was a wonderful lover. Maybe it was because I was really in love with him, because for me, he was always, without exception, a warm, caring and passionate lover.

He was a very good cook, too. His one-meal special was charbroiled steak, baked potato, frozen lima beans and a tossed garden salad. It was an unexpectedly delicious dinner. He made good coffee, too. I spent the night at the cottage because it was much too late to drive back to West Hollywood. I slept like a baby, warm and secure in his arms.

Staying at his cottage or his staying at my apartment became an almost everyday occurrence. The girls were allowed to spend every other weekend at home with me. David and I would pick them up at school on Saturday mornings, arrange fun things for us to do together, then take them back to school on Sunday evenings. It was mutual love between David, Kathy and Diane. I don't think the girls ever had as many good times with their real father as they did with David, who was a natural and loved playing the father role.

Our love was blossoming. Our arrangement was fine with me. Then one morning when I was leaving the cottage, his neighbors Richard Long, who was costar with Barbara Stanwyck in "The Big Valley" TV series, and his wife, Mara Corday, also in films, were leaving their home at the same time. Perhaps it was my imagination, but I felt the look they gave me was somehow demeaning. I had the most uncomfortable feeling, as though I were being caught doing something I shouldn't. Maybe it was because I had two young daughters, and the neighbors knew it. How would my children feel if they knew of my intimacy with David? They really loved him, but he was not their father. Kathy, especially, was old enough to suspect something, even though David never stayed over during the weekends they spent at my apartment.

To the neighbors, I tried to pretend I had just popped in for a while. Then I ran back into David's house. By this time I was crying. David couldn't imagine what had happened. As I began to tell him, I realized I wasn't fooling anyone. My car was parked outside his door night after night.

"I can't do this anymore!" I cried.

I poured my out my feelings. He knew I loved him and he had spoken his love for me, ever since that first night. Now, I had mixed feelings and, although he tried to comfort me, I ran out, got into my car and headed for home. I had to sort this out in my mind. I couldn't give him up, but I couldn't continue our relationship this way.

Tears blurring my vision, I could hardly see well enough to drive and through some miracle, I finally made it home. As I approached the door, I could hear the telephone ringing. I fumbled for my keys and rushed up the stairs. While I ran, I prayed: It had to be David, it just had to be. My heart was pounding as I raced to pick up the phone.

CHAPTER V

Ellie, it's me … there's only one solution … marry me!"
I couldn't believe what I was hearing. It was what I truly wanted
but didn't even dare to suppose. I was so taken aback I couldn't
answer, I was crying out loud, I tried to speak, but nothing came out
but my sobs.

Again he said:

"If you love me, please marry me."

"Of course I do! Of course, I will! I love you, I love you so!" I
shouted.

"Can I come over now?" He asked.

"Hurry, I can hardly wait for you to get here," I cried.

"I love you!" he shouted.

I sat down, holding the silent telephone. I was still clutching my
keys. I began to laugh and cry at the same time. I was overjoyed. A
giddy feeling swept over me and when I finally calmed down and
digested what had just happened, I ran to the bathroom to clean my
face and to treat my red and swollen eyes with ice packs and witch
hazel. I wanted to look especially good for him, my husband-to-be, the
love of my life. I did the best I could, but with the moments I had before

David arrived, I was trying on my new name, Mrs. David Janssen. Mrs. Ellie Janssen. How good it sounded. How right for me.

All the makeup artists in Hollywood couldn't have fixed me to look the way I wanted for David, but with my eyes swollen and red and my face puffy, now would be the true test. There was a sharp rap on the door. I opened it. We fell into each others' arms and held fast for the longest time, not saying a word.

"It took something like this to make me realize what an important part of my life you are. Let's try not to be apart ever again ... unless it's absolutely necessary!" he said.

"Not even then." I answered.

There was so much to do. David wanted to just run out and get married that same day. Although I would certainly have been willing, reason and practicality took command over our hearts.

I had not even met his family yet. He knew my children but had not met my family in New York. I knew they would all approve and be very happy for me, but, most important, the girls worshipped and loved him too.

I told him we should see his mother and get her blessings. We also had to notify his agent and studio and all his friends, many of whom I didn't even know. He took out a pen and grabbed a paper napkin, handed them to me, and said:

"You're in charge, make a list of everything we have to do, but make it short, I don't want to wait very long to make you my wife!"

I began scribbling; people to notify:

1. David's mother/family.
2. Kathy and Diane; mother, Ceil, Shirley, family in New York.
3. Agent and studio people.
4. David's friends, co-workers.
5. My friends, New York and Las Vegas.

David looked down at what I was writing and began laughing.

"I suppose you want to get married next year in a big church wedding, huh? Let's just do it, we can tell everyone later."

David called his mother and told her we wanted to come to see her. I don't know how much he had told her about me, we never discussed it, but she told him if he wanted to bring me for pot luck, we could join the family for dinner at seven o'clock.

When we arrived his sister Teri and his mother Berniece were preparing dinner in the kitchen. Jill, his other sister, came in and Berniece asked her to set the table. I could feel all of them scrutinizing me. It was a little uncomfortable, but I tried to remain poised. The table having been set, the food having been prepared in the kitchen, we all sat in the comfortable living room waiting for Gene to arrive from work.

"What a beautiful family," I thought. Their attitude toward me softened after a while. Little did they know what we were about to spring on them.

I couldn't help but notice that David was a little tense, and I'm sure his mother and sisters noticed as well. He was cracking all kinds of little jokes, trying hard to keep the atmosphere light.

Berniece asked a lot of questions. She knew David was seriously interested in me, and he undoubtedly had mentioned to her something about my daughters. She knew I had been married and was polite enough not to bring it up. Divorce was still uncommon then. Teri and Jill were both interested in Kathy and Diane and seemed genuinely eager to meet them. I was very candid with Berniece, answering all her questions, directly and to the point. I think she appreciated that.

Gene arrived home and shortly we all sat down to dinner. Gene had the look of a man devoted to his family, who worked very hard to provide a good home for them and was satisfied with the way life was going. He was very proud of David and looked upon him as his son.

The dinner over, we returned to the living room for coffee and pie. Then, David blurted it out:

"I hope you all like my bride-to-be. We're getting married!"

I was not expecting it to come out that way. I could see Berniece turn white. She obviously wasn't prepared for this announcement. There was a long pause, with Teri and Jill looking first at each other, then both looking straight at their mother, then at me, then at David.

I know they were all taken completely by surprise. Gene was the first to speak. He stood up, reached over the coffee table and shook David's hand:

"Congratulations, son. Looks to me like you picked a winner."

He then came around the table and gave me a gentle kiss on my cheek, saying, "You'll make him happy, I know."

David was beaming. Berniece appeared to have regained her composure, and said:

"Have you really thought about what you're doing? You've only known each other for a little while. Marriage is not to be taken lightly, I know, and you should know," she said, looking directly at me.

What she was really saying was that David was her only son, had never been married, and here I was a divorcee with two children. And what about his career? As if getting married would end his career and he would need to drive a milk truck to earn a living. That uncomfortable feeling was creeping back into my mind, but I really did understand her feelings, so I just smiled and tried to put on my best.

Teri and Jill seemed really excited about it and wanted to know when we were going to get married, whether our wedding would be in a church, would they get to come, would they get to meet Kathy and Diane then? So many questions, neither David nor I wanted to volunteer answers.

We assured Berniece that we had given serious thought to all things that matter and that the thing that mattered most was that we were in love. After all, I was sure that, as in the movies, love conquers all.

When David and I departed, I felt his mother seemed to be accepting the fact of our impending marriage, although somewhat reluctantly. Once in the car, David's comment was:

"Damn, I'm sure glad that's over."

We drove back to Beverly Hills, had a few drinks in the Polo Lounge, then went to my apartment for the night.

The next morning, Sunday, David called his agent, Stan Kamen of the William Morris Agency, at home. David asked him to come to the cottage for coffee at three P.M. He told Mr. Kamen he was sorry to bother him on a Sunday, but he needed to talk to him and he had someone he wanted him to meet.

Mr. Kamen arrived about twenty minutes late, which, David said, looking at his watch, "is about par for the course." David let him in. I was seated on the sofa. David sat down next to me and said:

"Stan, this is Ellie Graham, my fiancée, but not for long. We're getting married. We wanted you to be the first to know. How do you want to handle the studio and any publicity? We want a small ceremony, but we are willing to do it whichever way you think would be best."

Neither David or I were prepared for his reaction.

"YOU'RE WHAT? ... YOU ARE CRAZY! ... YOU CAN'T DO THAT ... NOT NOW ... MR. LASTFOGEL WON'T LIKE THIS ... WON'T LIKE THIS AT ALL ... DAVID, YOU CAN'T DO THIS ... YOU ARE IN A NEW SEASON ... IT WILL RUIN THE RATINGS ... IT WILL HURT YOUR CAREER ..."

Mr. Kamen bellowed, his face turning a bright red. David cut him off:

"Stan, calm down, hold on a minute." he said.

I suggested to David that I prepare to serve the coffee.

He nodded and I escaped to the kitchen. I was fearful. Would this cause David to have second thoughts? What about his career? Would our getting married really damage his career?

From the kitchen, I could hear them.

"THIS IS THE WOMAN I LOVE, I'VE ASKED HER TO MARRY ME ... SHE SAID YES, AND YOU'RE TRYING TO TELL ME THAT LASTFOGEL WON'T LIKE IT ... WON'T LET ME DO IT? YOU'RE THE ONE THAT'S CRAZY!"

"DAVID, YOU DON'T SEEM TO UNDERSTAND, YOU'RE STARTING A NEW SEASON, THE RATINGS ARE GOOD, GETTING BETTER ... BEING MARRIED WILL COST THOUSANDS OF FANS ... THAT MEANS RATING POINTS ... HOLD OFF A WHILE, THAT'S WHAT I'M TRYING TO SAY ... MR. POWELL WON'T LIKE THIS EITHER ... IT COULD COST THEM SPONSORS ... DAVID, WE ARE WORKING HARD TO BUILD A FOLLOWING ... THIS COULD COST YOU YOUR CAREER ... IF YOU ARE HAPPY BEING A NOBODY, FINE ... MR. LASTFOGEL WILL PROBABLY DROP YOU ... YOU HAVE TO THINK ... YOU'RE NOT THINKING NOW!" Mr. Kamen shouted.

David's voice was almost a whisper, but I could hear every word, very firm, very clipped:

"Stan, I don't understand this. I didn't expect this from you. I would think that you would be very happy for us. As I said, I'm getting married. You tell Mr. Lastfogel whatever. This discussion is over."

I heard the door close, and there was silence. I stood there in the kitchen for a few moments. Actually, I was paralyzed, holding a tray with coffee and three cups and saucers. Still no sounds. What was David doing? Is he coming into the kitchen?

Will he call out to me? I walked around the corner, down the steps, tray in hands. David was standing at the bar, pouring drinks. Mr. Kamen was nowhere to be seen.

I sat the tray on the coffee table, I stood there looking at David, fearfully. He looked angry, and until that point I'd never seen his anger. He turned, looked at me, held out a drink to me, smiled at me. He turned away, looked back seconds later, with an even broader smile, and spoke:

"Forget the coffee. He's gone."

I stood there with the drink David had just handed me, not knowing what to expect.

"A toast, to Mr. and Mrs. David Janssen!" he said, exuberantly raising his glass. I set the glass on the bar, put my arms around him, and let out a tremendous sigh.

I asked David who Mr. Lastfogel was. David said he was the head of the West Coast offices of the William Morris Agency, and had the power to drop him as a client. Of course, I knew that Mr. Powell was Dick Powell, the producer of "Richard Diamond," and a very powerful man in Hollywood. I asked him if he was certain about his decision, and would our marriage really hurt his career? He replied that all that he cared about was our happiness ... together.

David telephoned me from the studio Monday afternoon to tell me his mother wanted to give me a bridal shower. I wasn't really keen on the idea, but to start off our relationship right, I agreed. David said I didn't have to do it, but he agreed it would please her.

I asked David if he had heard anything from Mr. Kamen, Mr. Lastfogel or Mr. Powell. David said he had not heard a word, and didn't give a damn anyway. We were getting married.

The shower was held the following Saturday in Berniece's home. She had invited all her friends, ladies I had never met and wouldn't see again. Rita and Patty came with me so I didn't feel all alone. It was a congenial group. We received some nice gifts: linens, household appliances and a set of dishes.

Afterwards, Rita, Patty and I went to the Polo Lounge for a much needed hour of relaxation. I returned home to prepare for David when he would come from the studio.

We hadn't really set a date for the wedding, but I had the distinct impression from Berniece that she was taking charge of all arrangements.

When David arrived, we had a quiet dinner in my apartment. I showed him the lovely gifts, which he showed no interest in. When I told him that it appeared his mother wanted to arrange our wedding, he said softly, with a smile:

"No way."

On Tuesday I called all the people on my list. My mother and the rest of my family were all surprised and pleased for me. I called Sonny Small and Carmen Dell, my good friends from Las Vegas. I told everyone that we had not set a date, but it would be soon.

Sonny Small, who was in the chorus line at the El Rancho Hotel, spoke to the owner Beldon Katleman about our plans. She suggested we get married at the El Rancho. She called me back a couple of hours later and told me that Beldon offered to provide his bungalow for the ceremony, and would host a reception. He even offered to be David's best man. I had already asked Rita to be my matron of honor.

Time flew. It had been almost a month since David had proposed to me. I had done just about everything needed to prepare. I told David about Sonny and Beldon's offer, and he thought it was perfect. That way, we wouldn't have a big ceremony and see his mother crying. He hated to see a woman cry.

It would also preclude the press, and the studio could handle the announcement any way they wanted to — after the fact.

On August 22, 1958, Rita and her fiancé, David Chandler, flew with us to Las Vegas. We checked into the El Rancho. Another surprise: Beldon had arranged to have the Honeymoon Suite for us. We went to city hall and got our marriage license. I asked David if he wanted to change his mind.

"Not for anything," he replied with firmness in his voice.

The next morning, Sonny, Rita and Carmen were helping me dress. I had chosen a beige chiffon and wool tailored dress for the occasion. David looked sensational in his charcoal gray suit, white shirt, black silk tie and pocket handkerchief. The guests were all gathered in Beldon's bungalow, waiting for me. We were delayed because Sonny was searching for something blue, for the traditional "something old, something new, something borrowed and something blue." She found a piece of blue ribbon which I tied to an undergarment strap. It was both borrowed and blue.

I made a grand entrance, not because I planned it that way, but because of the delay. The ceremony was lovely and on Saturday, August 23, 1958 at two o'clock in the afternoon, I became the first Mrs. David Janssen.

The reception was wonderful. There were flowers everywhere, a magnificent buffet, a large wedding cake and plenty of champagne and other beverages. Beldon had invited many of the celebrities who were appearing on the strip. Don Rickles and Sonny King were particularly hilarious, making jokes about newlyweds and sharing in the merriment.

We retired to the Honeymoon Suite early, affirmed our undying love for each other and had a glorious night's sleep. Sunday, after brunch, we headed for the airport with Rita and David Chandler for our return to Los Angeles. David had to be back at work Monday morning, so the honeymoon was postponed indefinitely.

After David left for the studio around five A.M., I went back to sleep hugging his pillow. I awoke around seven, prepared my coffee and watched the morning television news. After taking a bath, putting on my makeup and dressing, I assessed the cottage. David had told me to make any adjustments I wanted to make it suitable for both of us, so I spent the entire day rearranging things. I made some sketches of how we could convert a large double bay window into a closet. There was just not enough closet space to accommodate both our wardrobes. The cottage was small, but held potential. That evening over dinner, I discussed the changes with David, and he was excited to know that we could make the cottage very comfortable for both of us.

I had brought with me my three prized possessions: my sewing machine, my dressmaker's dummy figure, and my professional hair dryer on a stand. I crammed them into a corner of the bedroom, because space was limited. We went to the hardware store and bought a rod to place across the bay window frame. I also bought print material and made drapes to cover the clothes from view, making a very economical and instant closet. The drapes complemented the decor and blended nicely with the solid beige drapes on the other windows. It was a modest home, warm and snug. But our domestic life was about to change.

CHAPTER VI

Just before Christmas, David and I were sitting on the sofa in front of the fireplace having eggnog. We heard rattling noises coming from the woodbin, which was built into the brick wall that covered the fireplace from floor to ceiling. When he went to investigate, a large rat jumped out. I got hysterical and he grabbed a poker iron to club it. No chance. It escaped back into the hole from which it came.

I couldn't sleep that night and I don't think David got much rest either. The next morning as he was preparing to go to work, he suggested I find an apartment for us in West Hollywood.

"I don't want to share our home with a rat, especially since the rat isn't paying part of the rent," he said.

I laughed, I loved his humor. He was not a storyteller, but he crafted hilarious one-liners.

With the first and last month's rent plus one month's security deposit being the standard required, we would need at least $1,000. My alimony had stopped and the "Richard Diamond" show still had not been signed for a full season contract. David was paid $750 per episode and the network was only doing about six episodes at a time. Money was very tight.

45

David told me not to worry, he would get an advance from the William Morris Agency. I didn't think they would advance him the money because they didn't want us to get married to begin with. He called me around ten o'clock and said:

"I have the money now, so find us an apartment. I trust your judgment."

I found a suitable apartment on Cynthia Street near San Vincente Boulevard. It had one bedroom, a den, two baths, a large living room, dining area, kitchen, ample closets and a balcony. It was on the third floor. It was only minutes from David's studio, a location he greatly appreciated. No more long commuting from the Valley to work. It was also close to everything we would need: supermarket, dry cleaners, restaurants, everything.

The cottage was on a month-to-month basis. Although we lost the balance of the rent for December, we didn't want to spend Christmas with the intruder, the rat. We moved into the apartment the same weekend. With a U-Haul, we made the move ourselves to save money. The bungalow had been furnished, so we had little to move. We had no cash on hand, but Sears, Roebuck and its payment plan enabled us to purchase our bedroom set and dinette table and chairs. Then, slowly, and somewhat piecemeal, we managed to make the apartment quite comfortable. We converted the den into a second bedroom with a queen-size sofa bed which we opened for the girls when they spent their weekends with us. It took several months to have our new place completed to our satisfaction, but it turned out well, and it was all ours.

While in this apartment, when we would have our little disagreements, David would vent his frustrations by putting his fist through a closet door. Because we couldn't afford to replace the door, I bought a dressing mirror and hung it over the damage. A few months later, he did the same thing to the bathroom door. I said to him, "David, if you keep doing that, we're going to run out of doors." We both laughed and laughed.

Another time, we had argued over something silly and, while sitting on the edge of the bed, I impulsively slapped his face. His automatic reaction was to slap me back! We looked at each other in shock; then be both broke into roaring laughter. Thankfully, neither slap was hard and we realized how silly we both had acted. Neither of us could have done something like that with forethought. We would spend two very happy years there.

David was still working long hours and he was so tired we would spend most of our time together in the apartment. Once in a while we would have friends over for a game of cards, but most of the time we just enjoyed being alone together, lying in bed watching television. The quiet in our lives was not to last.

When production on David's TV show went on hiatus in April, the sponsor, Ford Motor Company, wanted David in New York for some promotional activities. I was excited and looking forward to introducing David to my family. The trip to New York would prove to be our destiny.

After checking into the Plaza Hotel, we went to Danny's Hideaway, a very popular restaurant in Manhattan, one which I had frequented before going to the West Coast. We ran into an old friend I had dated back then, Wynn Lassner (nicknamed "Brownie") and Hy, a friend of his. They invited us to join them at Danny Stradellas' table at the Copacabana. East 46th Street was far too narrow to walk four abreast. Upon leaving the restaurant, Brownie and I walked together; David and Hy were right behind us. It was fun for me to show David a bit of my lifestyle in New York.

After the Copa, we went back to the hotel and no sooner did we arrive in our room, than David came over to me with tears in his eyes. He wanted to know if I really loved him or was I still hung up on Brownie. I was so amazed at the misinterpretation. Brownie was an exceptionally good-looking guy, and I realized that I had made a huge mistake showing any attention to him at all. I tried to reassure David of the love I had for him, but that made my heart ache to feel I had hurt him this way. It was my first insight into how sensitive my new husband really was.

It was on this trip that David was introduced to Henry Kalmer, a vice president of CBS Television. We were invited to the Kalmer's Park Avenue apartment for dinner on Friday evening, our last business day in New York. The Kalmers' were warm and friendly people, not too much older than we were. Both liked the "Diamond" show and thought David was a very fine actor.

During our dinner, Mr. Kalmer asked David how he was getting along with the William Morris Agency. David always spoke the truth, no matter what. He told Mr. Kalmer that he was not happy with the representation he was getting from the Morris people. He stated that Stan Kamen was upset about our marriage and David felt he was being held back. He also said he felt he should be earning far more than the "Diamond" contract was paying, considering it had been renewed and the ratings were high.

Mr. Kalmer asked David if he knew Abby Greshler. Of course, David knew his reputation as perhaps the most prominent agent in Hollywood but had never met him. David did not feel he was established well enough to be represented by a man of Mr. Greshler's stature.

After dinner, we were having coffee in the library and Mr. Kalmer asked David if he would like an introduction to Mr. Greshler. Of course! Mr. Kalmer placed a call to him in Los Angeles. After a few minutes of conversation, to our surprise, he handed David the telephone. I could not hear the conversation, but David had a big grin when he came back and sat down beside me.

"Mr. Greshler has invited us to his home for brunch on Sunday," he reported.

"That is great. You'll really like him and I'm certain he'll like you, David," Mr. Kalmer said.

Shortly after, we left their apartment for the short cab ride back to the Plaza Hotel. David was very excited. When we arrived in our room, David immediately called to change our airline reservations. He wanted to return to L. A. and prepare himself for this very important meeting.

The flight back was smooth. David was recognized by several people on the plane and many asked for his autograph. This phenomenon embarrassed David during the early years, but he was always polite and accommodating.

I could tell, the only thing on his mind was the meeting with Mr. Greshler. He knew that if Mr. Greshler would take him on as a client, our lives would change for the better. He was so right.

That Sunday we dressed carefully to make certain we would give the best impression. David was in his best black suit, white shirt, burgundy silk tie and matching pocket handkerchief. I wore a red, tailored two-piece suit with a white silk blouse and scarf.

We approached the massive wrought iron gates of Mr. Greshler's palatial Brentwood home. David was somewhat tense, apprehensive.

We parked in the circular driveway and rang the doorbell. The butler opened the door and escorted us to the expansive patio-pool area behind the home. Mr. Greshler was seated at a round table with telephones and a stack of business papers in front of him.

I think I was more nervous than David at this point. Mr. Greshler was of slight build with thinning hair and a pronounced overbite. He had a very white pallor for someone living in southern California. He stood when we entered, greeting us warmly but with an attitude which commanded respect. We sat down and the butler brought a tray of coffee. Sensing that David and I were both nervous, he tried to make us feel at ease by saying how lovely I looked and how handsome David looked.

He began immediately addressing the purpose of this meeting. He questioned David carefully about his background. He wanted to know as much about him as possible. His credits, including stage, TV, and film, his Army service and his experience with the Morris Agency. Then, the personal side of his life. Our marriage, children, was he a gambler, a drinker, everything. David answered quickly and to the point, which seemed to impress Abby Greshler.

He asked David for details about his contract with Four Star Productions. David told him the contract was short-term, with no guarantees, no perks, no benefits or security. He asked David how much he was paid. When David told him $750 per episode, he was astounded. He shook his head in utter disbelief.

"The Morris people must be a bunch of incompetents," he said.

David said he enjoyed working on the show, that in his opinion, it was produced well and the ratings were improving consistently. Mr. Greshler voiced his agreement. Apparently he knew all about us before we arrived. He had done his research. Then he leaned forward.

"This is a my contract. There is no negotiating it. You look it over, have your lawyer look it over, if you want me to represent you, sign it. I'll tell you only once and I'll tell you now, if you sign it, you must do everything I say and exactly what I say. Understood?" he said, handing David a thick stack of papers in a folder.

"Yes sir, but I don't have a lawyer. I can't afford one," David said in a serious tone.

Mr. Greshler smiled.

"Does this mean you'll represent me?" David asked.

"The first thing I have to do is get you released from the Morris agency. Then I can represent you."

"Thank you, Mr. Greshler, this means a lot to us."

"Please, call me Abby, and I'll call you David ... and I'll call your lovely wife Ellie, with your permission, of course," he said, smiling toward me.

Mr. Greshler was interrupted by the ringing of his telephone. After a short conversation, he turned to David, then looked closely. "You are on hiatus now, right?"

"Yes, until September 10th," David responded.

"Do you want to work now?" he asked.

"Yes, I need the money badly. We just recently moved to a new apartment. What do you have in mind?"

"Are you familiar with the stage play, 'The Gazebo'?"

"Of course. I know it well."

Mr. Greshler returned to the telephone and concluded his conversation, which neither David nor I could hear clearly.

"I'll have airline tickets delivered to you in the morning. A car will be sent to take you to the airport. You can take your lovely wife Ellie, but, unfortunately, not the children. You will have to be in Chicago tomorrow. Rehearsals start on Tuesday. It is guaranteed to run four weeks. You will have accommodations, a car for your use, $3,000 per week and one percent of the net receipts. It will be at the Drury Lane Theater in the Round. Tony DeSantis, a good friend of mine, is in charge."

"That's ... that's ... great ... uh, what about the Morris contract?" David stammered in astonishment.

"You don't talk to anyone. I'll take care of your contract with them and then I'll call you," Mr. Greshler retorted.

"I'll sign this now," David said, starting to sign the contract Mr. Greshler had given him.

"No, not yet. Wait 'til I have the release of the Morris contract. That can wait. I'll call you tomorrow."

The business over, we were ushered into the breakfast room where we met Violet Greshler, his attractive wife. We were served a light brunch. Afterwards, Mr. and Mrs. Greshler took us on a tour of their beautiful home. Abby was especially proud of his huge collection of mostly large, original oil paintings, in rich frames with individual lights over them. Abby bought paintings, some because they were aesthetically pleasing, and some for the value he believed they would have in the future based on the stature of the artist. Some were quite appealing. He had an eye for art.

David and I were both especially impressed with his private screening room. It was like a theater with a full-sized screen, and could seat many people. The chairs were comfortable easy chairs which could swivel. It had a large wet bar which spanned the length of the room on one side.

Violet showed me her closets. I was in awe. She had more clothes than most boutiques. She had exquisite taste, and I would join her at a later date for shopping tours in Beverly Hills.

We left their home around two o'clock. As we drove down the driveway, I squealed with delight and David let out a big "Wheee!" Neither of us had expected this turn of events. We had to pack and prepare for an early flight to Chicago the following morning.

In the car, David quickly calculated, $3,000 per week, plus one percent of the receipts;

"My God, Ellie, that's more than I earned in all of last year!" he exclaimed. I was delirious.

David had a strong background in performing on stage in small theaters and he enjoyed it. He knew the play, "The Gazebo," thoroughly and hoped he could do well in whatever role he was cast. I had never been to Chicago and was looking forward to the trip.

That evening, we went to LaScala for a celebration dinner. This was the start of something very, very big, and David knew it. The next morning we were at the airport at seven and checked in for our flight. We both felt exhilarated as the aircraft lifted skyward. I held tightly onto his arm as I watched the L. A. skyline disappear below.

We were met at O'Hare Airport by a limousine which took us to the Drury Lane Theater. On the top floor was our suite, which was large, tastefully furnished and comfortable. We unpacked and freshened up. The telephone rang and David answered. It was Tony DeSantis, the owner of the theater and the producer of the play. He asked if our accommodations were satisfactory, and David invited him to come up.

He did. He was an enthusiastic man and told us how much he admired David's work and how pleased he was to have David for the play. That is when we learned that David had the leading role. Mr. DeSantis assured David he would enjoy the experience, and told him there would be a cast meeting the next morning at nine. As he was leaving, he told us that if we needed anything, not to hesitate in calling him.

Chicago is a lovely city, especially in May. I was looking forward to exploring it, the museums, attractions and chic shops along the famous Michigan Avenue and State Street. David promised me that, with his first paycheck, I should go out and splurge on a new wardrobe. He knew how frugal I was.

The play was scheduled to open in one week. The following morning David began rehearsals. A car provided, the driver took me to Michigan Avenue. I asked him to come back for me in three hours.

The stores were fabulous and I was excited just being there. The city is so different from L. A. It is a mini-New York, in my opinion.

That evening when David came up to our suite, he was tired, but full of enthusiasm for the play. He showered and we were thinking about dinner when the phone rang. It was Mel Torme. He had seen the advertisements for "The Gazebo" and congratulated David. He said he and his wife Arlene were only in Chicago for a few days and would love to have us join them as their guests for dinner.

"What perfect timing," David told him.

They suggested we meet them at the Chicago Playboy Club, a beautiful and very festive place, with outstanding food and live entertainment.

Mel introduced us to Hugh Hefner, the Playboy founder. Everyone wished David much success in the play. It was a wonderful evening. We returned to our suite and retired early, around eleven o'clock.

David was working very hard. He was determined to put on his best performance by opening night, when the critics would be part of the audience. The play opened to a sold-out house. Everyone in the cast felt good about all the performances and anxiously awaited the morning newspaper reviews. Every one was outstanding, and David received glowing praise from three prominent critics. He was ecstatic.

Within a couple of days, the box office reported to Mr. DeSantis that sales were going at a rapid pace and he should consider adding a matinee on Saturdays. From the second week, every performance was sold out. Mr. DeSantis asked David if he would call Mr. Greshler to renegotiate his contract. David did not understand, but we soon found out why.

Abby called David the following evening before the performance. Mr. DeSantis wanted to extend the run of "The Gazebo" from four weeks to six weeks. David was deliriously happy and accepted instantly. Nearing the end of the fifth week, the play was extended to eight weeks, and shortly after, to twelve weeks. David was getting national attention for his magnificent portrayal.

David was now earning almost $6,000 per week and we had very few expenses in Chicago. We were building up quite a nice nest egg. Abby telephoned again and said he was flying to Chicago to see what all the fuss over David was about. He arrived and I accompanied him to the play on a Friday evening. Saturday, he joined DeSantis and us for brunch in our suite. Then he gave David his contract from the Morris Agency, quietly canceled, with no penalties. David's star was about to take a meteoric rise.

CHAPTER VII

David signed his first contract with Abby Greshler. After the signing ceremonies, Mr. Greshler looked at us and said, "David, I know you have worked very, very hard and will continue to work hard. You are very deserving of your success and you are fortunate to have a beautiful and supportive wife. From now on your star will shine bright."

"Thank, you, sir, that means a lot to us," David said, smiling and squeezing my hand warmly. Tony DeSantis congratulated us. It was a beautiful day.

We returned to L. A. at the end of August. We were sad to leave Chicago and all the cast members and the many friendships we had formed. We were, however, glad to be going home, and I was looking forward to spending time with the girls. They had spent part of the summer in New York with their father and were now back at Anokia School. "Richard Diamond" was to begin production within two weeks. David wanted to just stay at home with me and relax for that time.

We brought the girls home for the weekend, and I was glad to see how much they missed us. They wanted to know all about Chicago and, of course, "The Gazebo." I had clipped all the newspaper articles and reviews and the girls were very impressed to read about their stepfather. We had a nice Sunday together before I drove them back to school.

Monday, David had a meeting with Abby to discuss his "Diamond" contract. David wanted me to attend the meeting and he suggested the Beverly Hills Hotel for a lunch. Abby agreed, saying Frank Liberman, David's newly-hired publicist, wanted to do some photos for publicity on "Diamond," and said it would be a good backdrop for the photos.

When we arrived, Abby was already there. David was expecting a raise from Four Star Productions, from the $750 per episode to at least $1,000 per episode. Abby said he thought that might be possible, then he winked at me. I was impressed with the tone of this meeting; it was a real power lunch. I was also happy with the genuine concern Abby seemed to show for David.

David asked if he could attend the meeting with Four Star and the studio. Abby said he did not allow his clients to be subjected to the abuse of such meetings. However, just this once, he felt it would be good experience for David and he agreed.

Abby departed after lunch, and we were then joined by Frank, a photographer, and a writer from *TV Guide*. The photo session lasted about an hour.

The meeting with Four Star Productions, Universal Studios, Abby and David was set for Thursday morning. It appeared to me that David was very calm and prepared. He was confident that, with Abby, he would get what he wanted. I asked him to please call me the minute the meeting ended, that I'd be chewing my fingernails until I heard from him.

I heard the key in the door a little past three o'clock. David entered, hugged me, and Abby was right behind him. David asked me to bring out the champagne. They went into the living room and I brought out a bottle, bucket of ice and three glasses.

David poured carefully, then stood;

"A toast to the best agent in Hollywood, ABBY GRESHLER!"

"A toast, to a fine, rising star, DAVID JANSSEN!" Abby countered.

We raised our glasses and then I shouted;

"Will someone PLEASE tell me what happened?"

They both started talking at the same time, talking and laughing. Both were obviously excited and I couldn't understand either one. Then, David began telling the story:

"The studio was offering $1,500 per week, for thirteen weeks. I was ready to sign. Then, Abby told them he had prepared a list of what he had determined would be fair and equitable to all concerned. He passed the list around. I hadn't even seen it."

David took a deep breath, then continued;

"The head man shouted that they could not meet those demands because the network had only committed to thirteen weeks. Then, Abby stood up and yelled to me, 'Come on, David, we don't deal with liars.' — I almost fell off my chair. I didn't know what was happening. I thought this man just cost me my only job. 'Well, there goes the house,' I was thinking."

David took another deep breath.

"Then, Mr. Cohn, representing the studio, pleaded with us to sit down, he was sure we could work it out ..."

Abby continued, "I asked David to wait in the outer office, I know he didn't like that, but there was more haggling to do. You see, Ellie, what David didn't know, what Mr. Cohn didn't know, and everyone else in that room didn't know, is that I have been a programming consultant to CBS for the last few years. I've known for weeks that 'Richard Diamond' has been committed for twenty-six weeks, and they want David Janssen to continue as the star, so I gave them this list." Abby said, handing me a short piece of paper, in his handwriting:

JANSSEN:
a. $7,500 – wkly.   *c. Car.*
b. Dressing room/private phone.   *d. Health/hosp/life/ins.*

"Honey, you won't believe this contract ... seven thousand five hundred dollars per week, my own dressing room with a phone so I can call you on breaks, we get a new car too, plus expenses and health and hospital insurance for all of us, the girls too ... and life insurance on me!" David said, his voice rising with excitement.

Then David stood, picked me off my feet and gave me a big kiss, telling me how much he loved me.

With that, Abby headed for the door, he paused and said that Vi and he would be delighted to have us join them Saturday evening in their home for a screening of a new film. We instantly accepted, of course.

Alone, we were both jumping with joy. We had never dreamed of such a contract. There was no question, David Janssen was on his way to becoming a star.

We spent a quiet evening at home, celebrating with pizza and pop.

In the new season of "Richard Diamond," ratings started out high and continued to climb. This surprised the studio executives, but not Abby. It pleased David.

Frank Liberman, David's publicist, had launched a media blitz about a month before the season premiere. The blitz required numerous photo sessions, showing off his new bride at our apartment, at restaurants and of David on the set. Casual and candid photos along with feature stories appeared in fan magazines and TV sections of newspapers, nationwide. David was on the cover of *TV Guide*, and a couple of months later, the magazine did a feature story on Hollywood wives, where I was included. It must have worked. The ratings skyrocketed and Frank had proven himself to be a star publicist. He remained David's publicist until he married Dani Greco, who had him fired.

The success of the new season of "Diamond" put us on the "A" List in Hollywood. This meant invitations to several parties a month, in people's homes, restaurants and ballrooms. David was working very hard and was usually tired when he came home. The last thing he wanted to do was go to parties, so we only attended the ones Abby or Frank said were important. We had not become snobs as our close friends knew. And those in the business also knew and understood the work pressures on David. Besides, we were just basically homebodies.

When "Diamond" went on hiatus in May of 1959, David did not know if it would be renewed for the new season. The network had not made any announcements for their new lineup. Abby contracted for David to star in "Mr. Roberts" in a Dayton, Ohio theater, where the play was scheduled for an eight-week run. Of course, David wanted me with him.

Again, he performed to a packed theater at every performance. The reviews were outstanding. While in Dayton, we met Jerry Orbach, a member of the cast who also was a rising star. He had many fine starring roles on stage, such as "Carnival," "Forty Second Street," and "Promises, Promises." He is currently starring in the NBC TV series

"Law and Order," where he gives very realistic performances as a New York City police detective.

Jerry and his wife Marta introduced us to Dolores and Bernard Wolfe. Dolores, before her marriage to Bernie, had been an actress known as Dolores Michaels and co-starred in "Bus Stop" and many other major films. Bernie, who had written numerous books, many of them best sellers, had also been secretary to Leon Trotsky while Trotsky was in exile in Cuba.

David had read several of the books Bernie had written and was fascinated with his background. David held him in high esteem. He was delighted when the Wolfe's invited us to a dinner honoring Henry Miller, another writer David was in awe of, who wrote *Tropic of Cancer* and *Tropic of Capricorn* and a trilogy, among others.

David had fortified himself with several drinks before we arrived for dinner, and as usual continued guzzling Scotch to bolster his self-confidence when meeting such notables whose work he admired. There were no servants in the house. David kept the bottle of Scotch on the floor by his chair and kept filling his glass. Being somewhat intoxicated, he managed to put his foot in his mouth several times trying to keep up with these giants.

"Did you really screw all those women that you wrote about?" David slurred to Henry Miller.

"Certainly, the same as you killed your wife on 'The Fugitive,' " Henry replied with a smile.

We were the last to leave, and with Bernie's help, I managed to get David into the car at around two-thirty A.M.

The next morning David called Bernie and Dolores and asked:

"I know I screwed up with Henry Miller, but how many of your other guests have I alienated?"

"To tell you the truth David," she said, laughing, "I think we've lost all but our gardener."

I later found out that Bernie enjoyed David's humorous attempt at an apology.

Dolores recently reminded me of a week they spent as our guests in Palm Springs. We had recently employed a temporary houseman named Peter, who had a very thick accent. Dolores needed something ironed and asked Peter for the iron. Trying to be friendly and make small-talk, she questioned him about his accent. He told her he was from an aristocratic family in Poland, where they lost everything. Dolores then remarked; "How demeaning it must be for a Pollack like you to be doing this kind of work."

"Madam," he replied, "I am a POLE!"

Dolores hurried to tell us of her faux pas.

"Thanks a lot, Dolores," David said. "By Wednesday he will probably be on his way back to Warsaw with my whole damned wardrobe."

The next morning, while we were having coffee, David noticed the sugar bowl was a bit sticky. He said,

"I guess I'll have to fire that Pollack, after all."

Bernie laughed the hardest, maybe because he was part Polish.

Nicky Blair began as an actor in Hollywood but decided his fame would come in the restaurant business. He was so right. His restaurant on Sunset Boulevard still is a favorite haunt of many celebrities. David and Nicky were close friends. Before "Richard Diamond," David was a contract actor with Universal Studios. Nicky tells the story of David calling and asking if he could "sleep on your couch for a couple of weeks?" Of course, Nicky said yes. That two weeks lasted two and one-half years.

David's humor was constant. As Nicky tells it, one evening he had planned a "hot date." He was preparing a lavish home-cooked meal for the special lady. Even then, he had noticed that David was quite a drinker. Nicky looked all over the apartment for a secure place to hide a fifteen-year-old bottle of Chivas Regal Scotch. He had learned from experience that if it was available, David would drink it. He found nowhere safe in the apartment, so he went to the garage. In the loft he spied an automobile tire. He got the ladder and climbed up, placed the bottle in the tire well, put a wheel cover over the tire and climbed down the ladder.

He had asked David to stay away from the apartment that evening until at least midnight. The lady appeared, dinner was prepared, and the telephone rang. It was David.

"How's it going, Nicky?"

"Just fine, wonderful. You're not coming home are you?"

"No, no, just wanted to see how you're doing," David responded.

As dinner was nearly ready to be served, Nicky remembered the Scotch in the tire. He excused himself, rushed to the garage, grabbed the ladder, and climbed up to the loft. He reached into the tire, felt all around, but there was no Scotch! Instead, there was an envelope addressed to him. He climbed down, replaced the ladder, and opened the envelope.

"My Ginso friend, I, too, saw the movie 'Lost Weekend.' " It was signed by David.

It took Nicky Blair a couple of years to get even with David. Shortly after we were married, David, while on hiatus, was contracted to star in "Hell to Eternity" with Sessue Hayakawa. Nicky was also in the film. The film was shot on location in Okinawa at a Marine Corps base. The cast and crew were all put up in barracks on the base. The native girls were very friendly and somewhat loose. David proceeded to get very drunk. Late in the evening, Nicky and Sessue had to take David back to the barracks and put him to bed.

The following morning, over coffee in the dining hall, David asked:

"What the hell happened ... What did I do?"

As Nicky and Sessue looked at him grimly, Sessue began to "clap" his hands. Nicky said:

"You know, David, the reputation of these girls, some of them have the disease and don't even know it ... You better get checked out by the doctor before you go back to Ellie."

David's face turned ashen. Nicky and Sessue looked at him, then at each other, stone-faced. They could see David was becoming physically ill. David ran to the restroom. He returned there a few minutes later and was really sick. He still made the day's shoot.

It wasn't until they were on the return trip home that Sessue and Nicky told David the truth. They all had a good laugh. David could always laugh at himself.

For the two of us, there would soon be much we could laugh and be happy about.

CHAPTER VIII

The years 1959, 1960 flew past. They were glorious years with so many good things happening in our lives. "Richard Diamond" ended its run. David had mixed feelings about finishing the series, but was thankful for the much-needed rest. We had built a nice, though still small, nest egg, and money was no longer a problem.

David's vacation was short. He was in great demand and Abby arranged a guest star's role on "The Naked City," starring Paul Burke. That required our going to New York for two weeks. I remember the weather was cold and biting most of the time. There we formed a close and lasting friendship with Paul and his wife Peggy. Paul had been with David at Universal Studios and they knew each other fairly well.

Peggy and I would go shopping, take in Broadway plays and just run all over Manhattan while David and Paul were out playing cops and robbers. Paul and Peggy would eventually move back to L. A., and spend weekends at their second home in Palm Springs.

Abby also contracted David for several feature films. David was the star in "Hell To Eternity," "Dondi," "King Of The Roaring Twenties — The Arnold Rothstein Story," "Ring Of Fire," "Twenty Plus Two," and was in "Warning Shot," and "My Six Loves."

David felt unemployed every time the camera stopped rolling or the play ended its engagement. Then his insecurities would take over again, and, like all actors, he worried that he would never work again. I began to notice that when David wasn't working, he would drink more than usual, usually to excess.

He was not a mean or nasty drunk. He held his liquor well and seldom appeared drunk. Actually, he was rather charming, but he would get drunk at every opportunity. Fortunately, his star was still rising and he was always in demand, so he was never unemployed for long periods.

When money started coming in and finances seemed a little more secure, Fred Barman, David's business manager, suggested we buy a house instead of renting.

Trousdale Estates was the newest area in Beverly Hills and homes there were selling in the $100,000-and-up range. We found a mini-estate with a private road leading up to the house. It was not quite completed and we made a good deal with the builder. We arranged to finish the house ourselves because we had some of our own ideas we wanted to apply. We negotiated the price down to $110,000, inexpensive for the neighborhood, but a long way from the cottage we shared with a rat.

The basic house was sound and had all glass windows from floor to ceiling. The house faced the area where we planned to put our pool. It had three bedrooms, so we could have the girls live with us full time, three and a half baths, and servants' quarters. A huge parking area was imperative to allow us to entertain. We wanted to reciprocate for all the parties to which we had been invited.

We moved in to bare cement floors. We didn't have nearly enough furniture from the apartment and none of what we had would suit the house as I pictured it. We rebuilt the tacky laminated wet bar with fine French walnut paneling, a polished brass sink and antique brass faucets. We bought white Italian marble squares for the entry, den, bar area, and dining room and carpeted the rest. We enlarged the living room with two steps up to the new area and bought a baby grand piano for entertaining. None of us played piano. It was there for parties.

The master bedroom was large and had over twenty feet of closets along the hallway, but David needed that much for himself alone, so we added on a dressing room, closets and bath with a bidet for me.

David had his own rock steam room all done in marble. A cold water hose hung alongside the rock bin, which had glass sliding doors. The steam room was next to the already-installed large sunken tub. The girls' rooms were on the opposite side of the house.

All the houses in Trousdale had a Grecian flair, so one of my first projects was to do a sculpture of a Grecian woman for the back garden. I used our housekeeper, Edna, as a model. She was nearly six feet tall and had a striking figure and fine features. We received many compliments on that sculpture, and, to my knowledge, it even now stands in the garden today.

There was complete privacy because we were up on a knoll. The pool we put in was vast with three curved steps leading down into the water. On the opposite end of the pool was a fountain with water spilling into it continuously. The deck was large cement squares with smaller, diamond-shaped green marble inserts. I had balustrades installed around the trilevel concrete deck and the garden surrounding it, giving the deck a formal Old World look.

While we were making all the changes, Jack Stanley, our contractor, had the roof open in many places when a flash rain flooded the house. It never rained in September; this year had to be the exception.

The house was severely damaged and unliveable. We were up to our ankles in water and had to punch holes in the ceiling to keep the water from caving in the entire flat roof. Luckily, we were well insured and the insurance company put us up at the Beverly Hills Hotel in Bungalow Five, their biggest and best. It had three bedrooms, one for David and myself, one that Kathy and Diane shared, and the other for Beatrice our new housekeeper after Edna left. She didn't have to do much because room service was so handy.

For me, it was like being on vacation. David had to work, of course, Diane continued her classes at Beverly Hills High School, and Kathy went to work in Sy DeVore's new ladies department at his shop. Our stay lasted for well over a month.

We hadn't gotten that far into furnishing the house when this all happened, so that was my next venture. Jack Stanley had stayed on to help me with some of the interiors, like redoing the fireplace wall with French walnut paneling and making bifold doors in my combination closet and dressing room, which was about 30 feet long and 25 feet wide. I recall that finishing and furnishing the house cost an additional seventy-five thousand dollars or more.

I spent that money and the better part of the next year decorating, but it was worth it. I then put all my efforts into accessorizing it. David and I both appreciated antiques. Now we could afford them, within reason. Not only did they look good, but they also had potential as investments.

I scoured Los Angeles, discovering little shops and import houses in some of the most out-of-the-way neighborhoods. I was very cautious in my selections and made some very good buys on chandeliers, bronzes, wood carvings and paintings.

I also spent a tremendous amount of time searching for just the right fabrics for our window and wall treatments, and when they were finished, it was worth it. This was the first home we owned together and I wanted to make it a showplace. It was a labor of love.

My efforts worked. *Architectural Digest* photographed our home for their magazine, and I once again thought about how far we had come since we shared our tiny cottage with a rat.

Now, we could entertain.

It was during the filming of the "Richard Diamond" show that we met Fieldsie and Walter Lang. Walter was the very fine director who did some of the really big movies like "Can-Can." Fieldsie was the personal secretary and closest friend to the late Carol Lombard.

The Langs, writer Dick and his wife Mary, a relative of Clare Booth Luce, producer Milt Pickman and his wife, and Caesar Romero, all loved the game of poker. We joined the group and had weekly poker parties, most often in the Langs' home in Pacific Palisades.

Fieldsie's nickname for Caesar was "Butch" — what an incongruous name for the suave gentleman of films, who was every single woman's favorite escort. We all followed suit in calling him "Butch." He was a very good poker player and a lot of fun. Caesar Romero passed away this year, 1994. He had a grand life and will be sorely missed by those of us who knew him and the millions of fans to whom he gave so much entertainment.

The poker games were great. We'd all win or lose thousands of dollars, but settled at the end of the game for a tenth of that amount.

The liquor flowed, and Fieldsie would have her drinks mixed and served in a vase. This eccentricity pleased David because it allowed him to feel unrestricted in his own drinking. He kept up with her, drink for drink. The rest of us didn't keep that pace, but there was always so much food, we all overindulged ourselves that way as much as David and Fieldsie overindulged themselves with liquor.

We played at the Langs or at our place. We also enjoyed poker games with Peter and Edye Rugolo. He wrote the music for "The Fugitive" and "Richard Diamond." Others in the group were James Garner, Andy Williams and Claudine Longet, and Dick Martin.

Other than the poker games, we loved watching movies, especially when we would join Abby and Vi Greshler for screenings before the movies were released to theaters. Vi was always a gracious hostess and she would put out a big spread along with generous drinks and bowls of popcorn and candy. It was always a great assembly of people and a good way to relax. This comfort spoiled me for all time from going to public theaters.

We ourselves did some entertaining, mostly small gatherings of six or eight. Beatrice was a fabulous cook and Marshall Green was such a good houseman that we would "lend" him to our friends for their parties. Our big parties came a bit later.

In early spring of 1962, Abby sent a script to David, the pilot for a new series. David was happy with the challenge and the longevity it would provide. This would lessen his anxiety about spans of unemployment and his drinking. The creator was Roy Huggins, a highly-respected writer with "77 Sunset Strip," "Maverick," "Run For Your Life," and several other series to his credit. The producer was Quinn Martin, a super-star in the industry. He had produced such highly acclaimed series as "Twelve O'Clock High," among others.

David read the script and was impressed with the plot, but he was worried. He was concerned about the writers being able to continue with different story lines each week. In addition, the series was to be a weekly one-hour show. Most series at that time were half-hour shows, except for variety and specials. Even so, David felt the story line had good potential.

The pilot had been turned down by the NBC and CBS television networks. Then it landed at the fledgling American Broadcasting

Company. The dynamic president, Leonard Goldenson, was a man known for his extraordinary vision of what the television viewing public would enjoy. He commissioned the two-hour premiere and a full season's episodes. "The Fugitive" was on the run, and what a run it was to be.

CHAPTER IX

T he pilot was filmed in early 1963, and about August full production began. Again, Abby had negotiated a fabulous contract for David, including a large percentage of ownership in the series. The contract was so good that, to this day, I am reaping benefits from the percentage of ownership and residuals.

The pilot, written by Stan Whitmore and directed by the talented Walter Grauman, was filmed on location in Tucson, Arizona, with Brian Keith and Vera Miles as the guest stars. The cast and crew spent almost ten days in Tucson and returned to the studio to complete the interior set filming. In the final scenes of the show, David and Brian were to have a fight over a gun, and Brian was to throw David against a Greyhound bus at the terminal. Brian is such an intense actor, and he did the scene with such realism, that he bruised David's ribs.

The pilot aired in midSeptember of 1963, and we had a few close friends over to watch it. Of course, David and Abby had seen the daily rushes and the finished product. It was the first time I was able to see any of it. Naturally, I had read the script, but I was still mesmerized throughout the show. I felt positive it would be high in the ratings and a big success. David was pleased, too. David and I enjoyed watching all his shows. He said that while filming, he was too concerned with being in character and following the director to grasp what the finished product was like. When he did see the final version, though, he seldom found a scene that he wished he couldn't do over. He was a perfectionist.

The following day, we gathered all the newspapers and trade papers many from other parts of the country. Together, we read each one carefully. The majority of reviews were very favorable and there were many that were exceptional, especially about David's acting. He was such a fine actor and had prepared for the role so intensely that from the first episode you had to believe "Dr. Richard Kimble" was innocent.

At first, the series was filmed in black and white. Color filming was added much later when all the network stations were equipped with color receiving and transmission.

Little did anyone at the networks realize, but the first season of "The Fugitive" proved how much of a coup the series was for ABC. As the ratings grew, so did David's popularity. Fan mail was pouring in, bags full every day. We were forced to hire a secretary-Girl Friday, Geri Hockstetter. She was a dynamo and served us faithfully for two years, keeping up with the fan mail. It was a horrendous task, but one that David insisted on. Geri spent some of her time at the studio waiting for David to sign his photos and his notes to the fans. The rest of her time she worked at the house helping me plan our social calendar, which was growing enormously as well. David would bring home stacks of letters and read them in bed, scribbling notes for Geri to send to his fans. He was dedicated to them.

With "The Fugitive" in full production, David was working twelve to fourteen hours a day and missing dinners and social events. I had a lot of time to fill. I devoted it to my hobbies. I was still designing and making my own clothes. The dressmaker's dummy I brought with me when we first married was still with us. I would select my fabrics very carefully, make my designs, drape the dummy and sew, sew, sew. Each piece was an original. I never feared walking into a crowded room at some gala affair to find another woman wearing a gown like mine. David appreciated that my creations were far less expensive than those from some famous couturier. He would just beam when I received compliments on my gown, especially if it came from a woman. His pride in my talents only inspired me to make more.

I also enjoyed oil painting and sculpting. When David was studying his scripts, he was my model for the life-size bust I was doing of him. The likeness of him was uncanny. I wanted a mold made so we would have it for posterity, but, unfortunately, novice that I was, I took it to a place that used hot wax which melted the soft clay and distorted the features to the point of being unrecognizable. After all those months of work, I was devastated.

I encouraged David to try his hand at oil painting. He did one canvas which I thought was very, very good, considering that it was his first attempt. He went on to do several oil paintings of various sizes. Most were landscapes and seascapes. We gave them to friends who admired and enjoyed them. David would have periods where he would paint for a few days and then not touch a brush for months. It depended on his schedule and his mood.

He enjoyed athletics and sports, both as a spectator and participant. He was very good at tennis, but his high school knee injury would sometimes flare up, preventing him from playing for weeks at a time. He took up golf, but the project was pure comedy at first. David was ambidextrous. He was more proficient with his left hand, but began playing golf right-handed. He just couldn't get the little ball to go in the little hole and he would laugh and laugh at the wild directions the ball would take. He was convinced the clubs and the ball had a conspiracy against him. When he learned that he could buy left-handed clubs, his game improved considerably.

Golf had become such an integral part of David's leisure time, we were invited to join Arthur Fellows and his bride on their honeymoon. They had been engaged for many years, so it was not as if we would be intruding on their privacy. Arthur was in charge of production of "The Fugitive," and he and David had become close friends. All three of them were golfing addicts. I had little to do except wait for them to return for the evening festivities.

Based on the astronomical ratings of "The Fugitive," ABC renewed the show for the 1964–1965 season. Abby worked his magic and David was recognized by his peers as a superstar. This caused some personal inconvenience. The press demand for news about David, and our private lives, was unrelenting. Frank Liberman was bombarded with requests for interviews, photo sessions and gossip.

He was a master, being very selective in media coverage. David appeared on the cover of *TV Guide* six times, with eleven feature stories about him. David was becoming such a star, *TV Guide* even did a story on his mother.

Fan clubs were sprouting up all over the country. During the filming hiatus we were obligated to make a cross-country tour, making personal appearances in many cities, meeting members of his fan clubs and David appearing on local network affiliate programs to promote the series. The experience was exhilarating but tedious.

After the national tour ended and we returned to L. A., we received a call from the Burkes inviting us to their weekend home in Palm Springs. It was so relaxing, serene and private, that we decided to buy a place there of our own. It was on the 14th fairway of the Canyon Country Club Estates where we found our sanctuary. This spot would become our haven from the grueling tedium of L. A.

With Ruth and Milton Berle, we were among the first to purchase season tickets in the dugout of the new Los Angeles Dodgers' stadium. David loved baseball. We missed some games because of his working, so we shared our tickets with the Berles and other guests. Also constant spectators at the Dodgers' games were Cary Grant and Doris Day. We would all pack picnic baskets with cold cuts and delicacies and thermoses filled with cocktails.

We had met Barbara and Jackie Cooper through the Berles. The Coopers also had a home in Palm Springs at the foot of the mountains. George "Bullets" Durgom, a prominent agent in the business, was a neighbor of the Coopers, and Bill Bixby was their frequent house guest. With so many of our new friends there, we went to Palm Springs during practically all of our spare time.

Jackie Cooper had recently received his private pilot's license. David mentioned he would like to take flying lessons, and the next thing I knew, David and Jackie announced to Barbara and me that all four of us were buying an airplane and would no longer suffer the boredom of driving to Palm Springs.

They selected an Aztec twin engine, four-passenger plane. David began taking flying lessons. Flying was so much better than driving back and forth. It was also death-defying, with David and Jackie making the takeoffs and landings perilously close to the mountains. It was exciting, sometimes terrifying. We leased the plane to the Little

Santa Monica Airport when we weren't using it, and that way the plane almost paid for itself.

In fact, we started the trend for the Palm Springs/L. A. crowd of gathering at Matteo's Restaurant in Westwood every Sunday night. It was on the way from the airport and we chose it as our Sunday night hangout. Mikey, the maitre d' and brother of owner Matty, always held our table. The Coopers, "Bullets" Durgom, the Berles (who didn't go to Palm Springs every weekend), the Burkes, plus David and myself, made the stop a grand finale to our weekends. The Sunday trend, although with different faces, remains today.

In Palm Springs, David and I ran into Frank Sinatra at Ruby's Dunes restaurant. I introduced them, and Frank was added to our growing number of Palm Springs friends. Soon afterward, Frank married Mia Farrow, and the four of us would occasionally get together at Frank's Tamarisk home.

When in the Springs David played golf or tennis. At his urging, I tried my hand at golf. He bought me a beautiful set of clubs to encourage me. I used to play the 14th hole, in our backyard, over and over again. I took lessons and used to cart buckets of balls to the practice tee, but I couldn't get the hang of it. Consequently, I never joined the foursome because I didn't want to hold them back. Instead, I would lounge by the pool and all of us would meet at the country club for lunch. Occasionally friends would drop in at our house, and, of course, the bar was always open. Friday and Saturday evenings were almost always spent with friends.

Although Ralph Stolkin, a good friend, had a huge ranch house in Bel Air, he, too, would spend most weekends at his magnificent home in Palm Springs. The house was perched on top of a mountain peninsula on Southridge, an exclusive area where we eventually bought property to build our permanent dream home. Bob Hope would build his fabulous home across the way from Ralph's in years to come.

We would spend a lot of our time with Ralph and his other guests, including renowned actor Laurence Harvey. The pool at Ralph's was like walking into the ocean, with the water cascading over one edge, like a falls. Laurence Harvey would swim over the edge pretending to be falling off the mountain, but he would actually be standing on a ledge a few feet below. Harvey would often bring some of his cronies, and the pool parties would get quite risque, with skinny-dipping being the highlight of the evening, although Ralph, David and I were not participants.

Ralph Stolkin urged us to buy the property on the mountain peninsula right above his. It was about two acres, perfect for the home we were going to build. We hired Paul Giddings, an outstanding architect from Orange County. David, so impressed with Paul's designs, commissioned a scale model of the house at a cost of $10,000, so we could make any changes before construction began.

Christmas this year was extraordinary. We went all out. David began buying gifts early in December and hid them in his dressing room at the studio until the day before Christmas. Kathy, who was now working, bought extravagant gifts, fewer, but still extravagant. We gave Diane an extra allowance so she could participate in the gift giving.

Fortunately we had our secretary, who was a tremendous help to me. Not only did we have our family and close friends to select gifts for, but also various people who worked with David. There was also the Christmas card list. She hand-addressed and stamped nearly three hundred, a far cry from the thirty or so we sent in 1958, our first year as husband and wife.

We found the most perfect, biggest tree the living room would accommodate, a natural green pine that almost touched the nine-foot ceiling. What a wonderful time we had decorating that tree. We all pitched in for the trimming, even buying a stepladder for David, even though he was more than six feet tall, to place the angel on top by reaching into the upper branches. When the tree was finished, it looked like a poster ad, with an abundance of colored lights and shiny ornaments, some handmade by Kathy.

There were so many gifts, mostly from David, that they occupied at least one-third of the room under and around the tree. Nobody knew what was in them. We all had been quite secretive in wrapping them.

On Christmas eve, after trimming the tree and placing the gaily wrapped gifts around it, we all sat down to admire it and enjoy some eggnog, which David had generously spiked with brandy. Even the girls were giddy with delight.

We were all in such an elevated mood that David exclaimed, "Why wait ... let's open them now!" We scattered around the tree, passing packages to each other.

The packages that took up the most room was an eight-piece set of matching luggage by Koret, in pastel petit point bound in amber leather, for me from David. Kathy gave us a very unusual leather box that I still cherish. It stood on little brass legs with a brass handle on top. The rest of the gifts were equally exciting and useful, but in such an abundance it would be too difficult to remember or describe.

That New Year's Eve, we were invited to more important parties than we could possibly attend, but we didn't want to offend anyone. I suggested we have an open house which David thought was an ingenious idea. We had Geri Hockstetter send invitations. It was a wise choice. That way we would not be on the streets and highways, but in the comfort of our home.

That holiday season together was to be our best ever, before or, sadly, since.

David Janssen
Celebrity Photo Gallery

A star is born. David Meyer Janssen, all of six months of age, decked out in his pale blue China silk rompers.

At age 8, pausing from a stroll on his roller skates, David smiles for the camera.

David at the age of 12. His charisma definitely increased in later years.

Richard Diamond - Private Detective was David's first TV series. As these shots demonstrate, Richard Diamond had both a hard and soft side, shown with Barbara Bain (photo courtesy of Ann Mathis).

A composite of Ellie's modeling, 1957.

David and Ellie were happily married in a celebrity-filled wedding August 23, 1958 (photo courtesy of Ann Mathis).

In 1960, David starred in <u>Hell To Eternity</u>, featured here with Vic Damone, Patricia Owens and Miiko Taka.

The Fugitive featured numerous guest stars, even some whose staying power lasts until today. Kurt Russell played Lt. Gerard's son in two episodes.

Ron Howard, looking like a '60s version of Macaulay Culkin, huddles in his Opie-like charm.

David's career took off when he was cast to play Dr. Richard Kimble. The Fugitive pilot, "Fear In Desert City," was filmed in 1962 and aired a year later, launching TV's first one-hour series (photo courtesy of Ann Mathis).

David got a chance to have fun occasionally. In this 1964 photograph, he and Ellie cavort near the garden statue Ellie sculpted, using their housekeeper as a model.

David relaxing at home with a drink, a sight which became increasingly and distressingly all too familiar.

The Fugitive continued to bring numerous stars to the TV screen. In 1966, tough-guy Telly Savalas made an appearance in the episode "Stroke of Genius," just a few years shy of his *Kojak* days.

In 1967, sultry Suzanne Pleshette guest-starred in the episode "World's End." She would appear once more, two too many appearances for Ellie's taste.

On the set of the final episode of <u>The Fugitive</u>, a ratings record-breaking two-parter. Here are the three main characters: Fred Raisch as the one-armed man; David as Dr. Richard Kimble and Barry Morse as Lt. Gerard (photo courtesy of Ann Mathis).

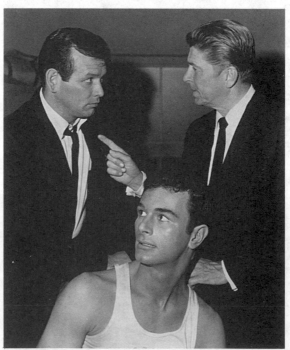

David, with future U.S. President and Bonzo star, Ronald Reagan and Charles Knox Robinson appearing on CBS-TV in a General Electric Theater production, <u>Shadow of a Hero</u> (photo courtesy of Ann Mathis).

While Dr. Kimble was being retired, David's career stayed on a fast track. That same year he appeared in <u>The Green Berets</u> with "The Duke," John Wayne.

David and Anthony Quinn in a scene from <u>Shoes of the Fisherman</u>, filmed in Rome, 1968.

Goofing around before the band in 1969, from left to right: Jackie Cooper, Chuck Connors, Quincy Jones, Mike Douglas and David.

David always seems to be with an attractive woman, whether on or off stage. Here he is with Big Valley's Barbara Stanwyck.

A dapper David with anyone's dream prom queen, Raquel Welch.

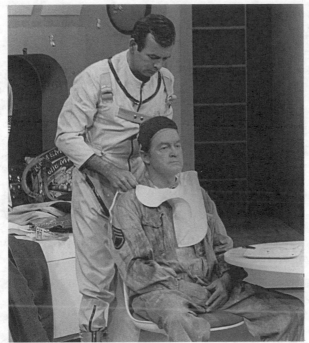

David and Bob Hope are the "Odd Astronauts" on <u>Chrysler Presents Bob Hope</u>, a special on NBC-TV, October 14, 1968.

Dean Martin and David "hoofing" on Bob Hope's TV special.

David, looking like James Dean, alongside his 1969 Rolls Royce Corniche convertible, photographed during his 1970 divorce trial filed against Ellie.

Also in 1970, David and film hunk Gregory Peck were together in <u>Marooned</u>.

David made a guest appearance with William Conrad in a 1973 episode of <u>Cannon</u>, a Quinn-Martin Production.

Carol Connors, songwriter, with David. They collaborated on writing *My Sensitive, Passionate Man*, a song for an NBC movie of the same name. The song won an Emmy in 1977 for Best Theme Song.

Harry O co-star Anthony Zerbe, who played Lt. Trench, and David. Anthony was admired by David and enjoyed working with him. *Harry O* was David's last TV series.

Mike Douglas clowning with David on TV's *The Mike Douglas Show*, October 25, 1976.

Ellie Janssen, always at David's side, reflects by his star on the Hollywood Walk of Fame.

CHAPTER X

When David went on hiatus, the timing was perfect for us to join Ralph Stolkin as his guests, along with dancer Cyd Charisse, her husband singer Tony Martin, and Bernice and Sidney Korshak, on an ocean voyage to London.

It was to be a wedding party. Ralph was to be married to a daughter of the Wolfson's, a very prominent family in England. Unfortunately, the wedding never took place. Crossing the Atlantic on the United States Line was pleasurable, however. The ocean voyage was David's first and he enjoyed it immensely.

We stayed at a small but charming hotel, The Connaught, in London, where the rooms were individually decorated with authentic antiques that added to the lodging's warmth. There were gated, open elevators with white-gloved operators, huge bathtubs with heated towels and large terry cloth robes. The dining room was known for its excellence in food and service. It was an absolute delight.

About a week later, Sidney had to return to New York. Bernice stayed on with the rest of us and we flew to Rome. There we stayed at the Excelsior, a very, very elegant hotel. Cyd, Bernice, and I went on a shopping spree and the men did their own thing. We met them later at Piccolo Mondo at cocktail hour for drinks and dinner. Rome was delightful with all its fountains, statues and little outdoor cafes. It was where David learned to love fresh raspberries that tasted as though they just came out of the garden. We all ate well in Italy, where the local food is quite delicate, not heavily spiced as is the American version of Italian food.

At one of the cafés, Ralph picked up the check while David and I both noticed the looks that passed between Cyd and Tony. But Tony didn't reach for his wallet either. When David and I discussed it later, privately, he mentioned that he felt it would be embarrassing and an insult to Ralph, our host. David was never stingy; he was always picking up checks. He hated the idea of being considered a moocher.

Madrid, Spain was our next stop, the place known for bullfights, not for food. Our experience with both was mixed. We visited a friend of Bernice Korshak's on Costa del Sol, who set up a beautiful lunch for us. It was the first time I ever tasted gazpacho, and I loved it. Another time at a small restaurant, however, we ordered scampi and the shrimp arrived with eyes staring at us and feathered tails, UGH!

We spent about five days in Madrid and went to the bull fights. I couldn't stand to see the picadors heaving their darts at the poor bulls. I know the bulls are bred for this purpose, but I wish they weren't killed. The toreador was magnificent, though. Sometimes he would daringly turn his back to the bull; then, with breathtaking grace and power, swing his body and cape back around to face the animal just as the bull was charging.

The last morning in Madrid, as we were all preparing for our departure to the United States, David left the room before I was even dressed and paid the total bill for all six of us. He never did anything in a small way.

When Ralph found out, he told David in front of the group, "You're my guests and that was entirely unnecessary." David, like Ralph, was accustomed to doing things on a grand scale.

We returned home and David was anxious to get back to work. Although I did not realize it at the time, the stress of "The Fugitive" was taking a toll on him. He began drinking more and more, although always off the set. Now he would have three or four drinks before dinner, which he never did before. This began to disturb me.

The filming of "The Fugitive" was always set at a fast pace. To shoot a one-hour episode normally required eight to ten working days. Each day was close to twelve hours. Many factors played a part; the weather, the lighting, the times of day for a specific scene. It put a lot of pressure on David, because he was in almost every shot.

In addition, the location shootings for the series required us to travel extensively. We crisscrossed the country. It was hard, but we really enjoyed it. It gave the fans in small towns and big cities alike a chance to watch the filming, some even to participate as extras, and a chance to see David Janssen in person. The publicity was great for the ratings too.

Quinn Martin hired the very best writers and directors for "The Fugitive," and their overall quality amazed David. The scripts were excellent. Most of the directors were great, with a knack for being clear and precise and the ability to put the entire cast in just the right frame of mind for each scene.

Quinn's choice of the cast helped the continuing success of "The Fugitive," whose prominence drew top-name guest stars, such as Sandy Dennis, Frank Sutton, Bruce Dern, Susan Oliver, Ed Nelson, Joanna Moore, Kevin MaCarthy, Richard Anderson, Telly Savalas, Robert Duvall, Ruby Dee, Joan Collins, Linda Evans, Angie Dickinson, Richard Long, Ed Asner, Kurt Russel, Robert Culp, and many, many more. Of course, the narrator was the gravel-voiced William Conrad, who would later have his own series, "Cannon," also produced by Quinn Martin. Barry Morse played the relentless "Lt. Gerard."

James Farentino was hired for one episode and he and David hit it off. During the filming, we had dinner with Jimmy and his fiancée, Michele Lee. Over the years we would become very close. Jimmy would go on to become an outstanding actor and Michele's career has sky-rocketed with her role on "Knots Landing," television movies and specials.

David seemed happy even though the pace was even more grueling than the previous season. We had been married for almost seven years when the first hint of suspicion clouded my bliss.

Suzanne Pleshette was hired as a guest star, cast as a girl from the home town of Dr. Kimble, a woman who was madly in love with him whether he was innocent or not. She offered to help him evade capture while scheming to keep him with her. Her role name was "Ellie." Her hair style was very similar to mine. Her voice was sultry.

I did not go to the set for this episode because my mother was visiting us from Florida. The last night of my mother's visit, David called home around five o'clock to tell me he was working late and not to hold dinner for him. He told me he had a few more scenes to shoot. Of course, I thought nothing of it.

About eleven o'clock he called again. It sounded as if he had been drinking. He asked me to meet him at the LaScala restaurant immediately. "How nice," I thought. "We will have a late snack together."

I was wrong.

When I arrived at LaScala, David was sitting in a far corner booth. His head was down on his arms which were sprawled on the table. I thought about how tired he must be. I kissed him gently on top of his head and sat down. He looked up and smiled. He ordered us both a drink and asked if I was hungry. I told him I was not, but he should eat if he was.

"Ellie, I had dinner. I had dinner ... at Matteo's ... with Suzanne Pleshette. I wanted you to come here so we could talk ... so I could tell you about it before you read it in the papers," he said. His voice was tense.

"But, I thought you had to finish shooting," I replied. I was somewhat bewildered by what he was telling me.

"We finished, I took her there for dinner. It's that simple," David stated.

"So, what does that mean?" I asked.

"It means nothing ... absolutely nothing ... I just didn't want you to read about it in the papers ... you know how they lie ... I don't want you to think something about nothing!" He said, his voice rising. He was showing signs of anger, perhaps mixed with guilt.

"Darling, I don't think anything wrong, I'm glad you told me, but you could have told me when you came home. Why did you want me to come here?" I asked, looking into his eyes, stroking his hands.

"Because I wanted to tell you now and I want you here now, with me ... Anything wrong with that?" he asked.

"No, there is nothing wrong. Can we finish our drinks and go home? You've had a long day and you look so tired," I responded, thinking how drunk he was.

We sat in silence sipping our drinks for quite some time. David kept ordering more drinks. I did not want to say anything. I did not know what to say, not understanding what was going on with him. He was getting very drunk. Choosing my words carefully, I suggested we go home and have a nightcap in our room. He agreed. I convinced him that we should leave his car in the parking lot and I would take him to get it in the morning. Again, without any argument, he agreed. That was unusual, because David would never admit he was too drunk to drive.

Driving home, I was in a total state of confusion and fear. Was David tiring of me? Was his love for me fading? Was I losing him?

It was almost two o'clock in the morning when we arrived home. The house was dark except for the light in the foyer. I was relieved. David had fallen asleep in the car. I gently awakened him and helped him into the house, then down the long hallway to our bedroom. I somehow managed to get him into bed and removed his tie, jacket and shoes. I loosened his belt, covered him and then crept into bed beside him. I cried myself to sleep, with all the questions raised by the previous hours tearing through me.

My mother was returning to Florida the next afternoon. I was glad of one thing: She wouldn't have to see or suspect anything was amiss between David and myself. I let David sleep until he awoke of his own accord. I was preparing to take my mother to the airport and brought David his coffee and orange juice before I left. He pulled me onto the bed and kissed me. He looked into my eyes and said, "I love you." I was still bewildered, but I felt somewhat reassured that maybe I was wrong about the night before. I told him I would be back from the airport as quickly as I could and we could relax and talk. He insisted on coming out to say goodbye to mother.

My mind was racing as I drove back from the airport. I had so many fears, doubts, even some anger. I was at a loss trying to get control of my feelings, not knowing what was really going on. I had never doubted David. I never had any reason not to trust him completely.

Something kept gnawing at me, tearing at my heart. Was Suzanne Pleshette trying to steal my husband? Was David falling in love with her? What was going on? I couldn't figure anything out, but I was determined to talk to David and get to the bottom of it.

When I arrived home, David was refreshed and sitting on the patio in his robe. He was having a Bloody Mary. I took his hands and looked into his eyes.

"David, I love you ... more than you'll ever know ... what's wrong with us?" I pleaded.

"Ellie, honey, there is nothing wrong. I'm sorry about last night. Nothing happened between Suzanne and me, there were some photographers at the restaurant and I just felt I should tell you I had dinner with her ... that's all ... I didn't want you to see it in the papers and think something was going on," he replied.

"O-k ... I'm sorry ... if I doubted you," I said, still unsure.

"Fine, can we forget it now?" he asked.

"It's forgotten," I lied, trying to smile.

He pulled me onto his lap and kissed me, and I put my fears aside for a while.

Over the next few weeks it became apparent to me that David's drinking was increasing even more, and it began affecting his personality. He became moody and quick-tempered. I was very concerned. One evening he came home very late from the studio, even though I knew they had completed the day's shooting hours before.

David said he had a few drinks in his dressing room. As he was preparing himself another drink, I said:

"David, don't you think you've had enough?"

"No, and I'm going to have more."

One thing led to another and he stormed out of the house. I heard his tires squealing as he went barreling down the driveway. I was very worried. He shouldn't have been behind the wheel.

"Suzanne Pleshette," I thought. She was living at the Doheny Towers at that time. I called. When she answered the phone, I blurted out,

"I think David is on his way to you. When he gets there please, please, please, don't let him in,"

"I'm sorry, I can't help you," she replied coolly, hanging up the telephone.

Then I realized that all I was accomplishing by calling her was to give her notice to fix herself up for his arrival. In my panic and fury, I jumped in my car and drove down the hill to see if he was at her apartment. Sure enough, his car was in the open garage. I went to the concierge to inquire which apartment she was in. I was going to confront them both.

"I will have to announce you, madame. No one is allowed up without being announced."

I stood there confused. I thought of calling the police, but I knew they wouldn't help.

"Oh my God," I thought. "How could this be happening to us?"

I returned home to spend miserable hours waiting for him.

When he did return home, we didn't talk. I didn't know what to say or how to handle the situation.

The following morning over coffee, he looked at me sheepishly and said:

"I needed someone to talk to and she seemed a good choice. She thinks like a woman and I thought maybe she could give me some advice," he said.

Wanting to believe him, I accepted his explanation and forced myself to suppress my doubts and live as if nothing were amiss between us.

On appearance, there really didn't seem to be anything for me to worry about. I knew that when he wasn't at work, he would be home with me. The only thing that was really bothering me was his drinking, and I believed that it was a direct result of the pressure of work.

Sometime later, we were invited to dinner with Cluney and Jimmy Komax, a comedian who later became a successful director, and Barbara Cooper. Jackie was out of town. We all went in Barbara's car. After dinner, Barbara was driving us home. The Komaxes were in the back, Barbara was driving, and David sat between Barbara and me. He'd had quite a few drinks at dinner and I just wanted to get home.

As we were nearing Trousdale, David leaned over to kiss me. I never kissed with my eyes open, but something just made me do it. I saw David's hand reaching under Barbara's skirt. I was shocked and livid! I let him know in no uncertain terms what I thought of his behavior. I shouted some obscenities, normally foreign to my tongue. He chuckled and flashed his boyish grin, though his drunken stupor did not abate my anger.

"What's come over him? What's happening to David?" I thought.

If the Komaxes or Barbara had any reaction to the scene, I was too furious to notice.

My sudden mistrust of David was justified by the next blowup we had. During a shouting match, I lost my voice completely. I tried to speak, but no sound would come out. David stormed out of the house.

"Suzanne Pleshette," I thought.

I jumped in my car and barreled down the hill to see if he was at her apartment. His car was not in her garage or in the vicinity. I drove around aimlessly. Then I thought maybe he went to the Coopers'. As I approached their house on Rodeo Drive there it was, his car, parked right in front. The house was dark, except for a light leading upstairs. I leaned on the bell, it rang steadily. I yelled out looking through the narrow glass panes on each side of the front door:

"DAVID ... I KNOW YOU'RE IN THERE!"

After what seemed a very long time, which may have been only moments, I saw Barbara run up the stairs in a scanty baby doll nightie. A minute or two later, she came down wearing a floor length muumuu. As she opened the door, I could see David coming from the darkened living room, tucking his open shirt into his trousers.

"WHAT'S GOING ON HERE? WHAT'S THE MATTER WITH YOU, DAVID?" I implored.

Barbara said something like, "We were just talking," but that's not the way it looked. Then I said, almost as if I were speaking to a child,

"David, are you coming home, now?"

He picked up his jacket and without a word, he left with me. I followed him home.

If only we had been able to communicate. I didn't feel I could confide in anyone. I telephoned Jackie Cooper in his office the next morning after David had left for work.

"Jackie, please come over right away, it's urgent!" I implored.

I told him the whole story, in detail, about what had happened the night before. There was a look of disbelief on his face. He said, "That just can't be ... not Barbara ... not David."

He looked at me as if he thought I were making up a story he didn't believe. It only frustrated me more. I couldn't even talk to him about it, to try and straighten the situation out.

I had thought that because he was David's good friend, maybe he could help David. Instead, that was the end of my friendship with Barbara and Jackie Cooper.

From here on, I couldn't believe anything. I found my lack of trust overpowering my every thought. If he was an hour later than I expected him from work, my suspicions were aroused. I found myself calling the studio more often, checking on him and hating myself for it. Our marriage was sliding downhill — fast.

CHAPTER XI

After the incident with Barbara and Jackie Cooper, I suppressed my emotions, convincing myself that I would only make matters worse by letting my suspicions run rampant, or confronting David with every dark thought.

I forced myself to pretend we were newlyweds again, as if nothing had happened. It worked — for a while. I felt I had done the right thing. David came to me a couple of months later and told me he was seeing Dr. David Ruben, the famous psychiatrist who would in years later find fame with his book "Everything You Always Wanted To Know About Sex ... But Were Afraid To Ask."

I had no idea David was seeing a psychiatrist. I had noticed that he had slowed down on his drinking considerably. We were talking more openly. I thought it was my change in attitude that was helping us. David told me the doctor suggested it would benefit our marriage if I were to see him as well. I agreed. I would fly down from Little Santa Monica Airport, or, if the plane was busy, I'd fly Pacific Southwest Airways to Dr. Ruben's office in San Diego. I would see him one day during the week. David would see him on Saturdays. We each had two-hour sessions.

Our visits to Dr. Ruben would last almost two and a half years. In retrospect, I think it did more harm to our marriage than good, though it certainly helped my mental state at the time. Dr. Ruben's wife had borne their first child, and the doctor was constantly raving about his new baby boy. This constant harping, I feel, had an influence on David's desire to have his own children. He encouraged me to have the hysterectomy Dr. Krohn eventually recommended, saying we had Kathy and Diane and he didn't want more children.

However, for quite a while I thought our sessions were helping and that our home life was less stressful.

Then Suzanne Pleshette was hired back to do a second part of the earlier story-line for "The Fugitive." When David told me, I was furious, not with David but with Quinn Martin. The following morning I telephoned Quinn at the studio. I began calmly, asking him why he hired her back.

"You're not showing me much consideration. What are you trying to do, cause us to divorce?" I wailed.

We ended up cursing at each other and he hung up on me. I told David about the call when he returned home. He had already heard about it. We didn't discuss it further.

It was at that time that David revealed to me that it was Suzanne who had recommended Dr. Ruben to him. Perhaps David was telling the truth, perhaps he and Suzanne were just friends, because they never gave me any reason to be suspicious again.

Diane was almost seventeen and becoming surly. Kathy told me that Diane had confided that she thought she was pregnant, a fact which might have accounted for her recent moodiness and rebelliousness. I knew she was seeing a boy from high school, but I never thought things had gone this far.

I arranged an appointment for her with my gynecologist. He confirmed our suspicions. We discussed it very carefully. David and I told her how much we loved her and would do anything in the world to help her. It was her decision not to carry to term.

It seemed best for Kathy to take a couple of days off work to escort Diane to Tijuana, Mexico for the necessary operation. If I were to take her and we were stopped along the way, it might have aroused suspicion and David's name would naturally be exploited.

When Kathy came back from Mexico, her attitude had not changed much. If anything, she was less communicative than before. She ended up running away and we had to call the police to help us find her. She got along famously with Berniece, David's mother, so it was decided she would live with her. I transferred her child support from her father to Berniece to cover her living expenses.

Geri Hockstetter decided to move on, and we were sorry to see her go. Her replacement was Victor Gentile. He was very efficient and was more than a secretary; he was my right hand. During my tough times with David, Victor's sense of humor lifted me out of the doldrums and kept me laughing. He was a great asset. He helped me get Kathy into her own apartment.

Kathy was now working at a graphic arts company in downtown Los Angeles. We were able to rent a darling little Westwood cottage owned by Nicky Blair. Kathy could afford the modest rent, and I helped her decorate and get settled in.

With our plans to build our permanent home in Palm Springs in high gear, David and I decided to sell the Trousdale home and lease an apartment in the new high-rise, The Sierra Towers, at the foot of Trousdale Estates on Doheny Road. We could stay there when David was working. We converted the second bedroom into a closet just for him. With all the clothes he bought, he would need every square inch.

It was my own fault. I had encouraged him to loosen up, to get away from just wearing his usual conservative look. He took by advice, but, as usual, to extremes. If he liked a sweater, he would buy a dozen. If he liked a suit, he would buy several. David didn't understand the meaning of moderation, whether it was in drinking, buying clothing, working, buying gifts, or any other part of his life. He was a man of extremes, no matter what he did.

We had been in the Sierra Towers for several months. One evening Michele Lee and Jimmy Farentino came to visit and told us that their good friends, Dani and Buddy Greco, lived two floors above us. She called them and we were all invited up for cocktails. Years before, Dani and David had been under contract at Universal Studios at the same time. I had known Buddy from Las Vegas. It was like old friends getting together again.

Living so closely to each other, we naturally spent a lot of time together. Dani, being a fabulous cook, frequently made dinners that we all enjoyed together. We were seeing less of our other friends because it was so convenient to just pop upstairs or for them to run down to our place. I found out recently, that Michele's feelings were hurt because we were seeing less of her and Jimmy and more of the Grecos.

Also living in the Sierra Towers were Patty Duke, as well as Babs and Willie Shoemaker, one of the world's most famous jockeys. No wonder the tabloids would later call it "Heartbreak Hotel." All of us ended our marriages, sadly, in divorce.

It was David's decision to bring "The Fugitive" to an end. After four grinding years, he was tired of "running." The studio wanted to continue, saying they could keep the scripts going, but David insisted and they finally relented.

When production ended on "The Fugitive" in the spring, we went to the Virgin Islands to visit my good friends from years before when I was still in New York, Louise and Elliot Fishman, who had a mountaintop estate in St. Thomas. We had only been there a few days when Abby sent David the script for "The Green Berets," starring John Wayne. The script called for David to play the role of a journalist, disliked by all the military officers. David was not interested in the script at all and did not want to do it, but Abby convinced him he should. We cut our vacation short, which was disappointing to both of us.

We returned home and David left for location shooting at Fort Benning, in Columbus, Georgia. David found John Wayne to be as his legend describes, the ultimate actor. But not always a gracious person. One day, the Duke lost his temper with a young Oriental extra on the set and was berating him loudly. David intervened. The result: He and John Wayne had a heated argument and David walked off the set, something he had never done before in his career.

I visited David in Columbus for a few days. I was being treated by Dr. Rex Kennamer, the famous diagnostician, for many months, for what he suspected were allergies. My eyes were swollen and in a constant state of tearing. I had painful, blurred vision. I quickly returned to L. A. to see Dr. Kennamer because my eyes started to bulge. I asked him if it could have anything to do with my thyroid, because there was a family history of such problems.

He sent me to Cedars of Lebanon Hospital for tests. An intern took one look at me and said he knew, without tests (although tests were done) that I was suffering from a hyperactive thyroid as a result of shock and stress.

Dr. Kennamer then prescribed medication to treat the problem. After being on medication for a couple of weeks, I was feeling much better and my condition improved. Peggy Burke and I decided to spend a four-day weekend in Las Vegas, and I told David when he called from Columbus.

To our amazement, David arrived in Las Vegas the night after Peggy and I did.

"I wanted to surprise you. I missed you terribly," he said, after hugging and kissing me.

David, never one to do things halfway, had chartered a Boeing 727 airplane and invited quite a few members of "The Green Berets" cast and crew, including Eddie Donno, an actor and stuntman, to come along.

He also brought Irene Soo, one of the female leads in the film. She would play an integral part in the breakup of Eddie's marriage to Kay, who would later become one of my closest friends.

The weekend was full of fun and spirits. I hated to see it end. David received a call from an irate Mervyn LeRoy, the director of the film, giving him flack for taking "half the crew" with him, so David sent the crew and cast back to Columbus Sunday night while he stayed over an extra day with me. He left on Monday evening and Peggy and I returned to Los Angeles, where I remained until he completed the film.

David was invited on a safari to Kenya, Africa as a guest of ABC Sports. This made me feel left out because I wasn't asked to accompany him. He suggested we go to St. Thomas to continue our vacation, which had been cut short by "The Green Berets." Then he could go on to Africa, when we changed planes in New York.

The last two episodes of "The Fugitive," titled "The Judgment," would be aired on August 22 and August 29. When I told Louise and Elliot, they decided to host a party in David's honor and invited many of the most prominent people living on the island. They thought it would please him.

The day of the party, he wanted to go into town to buy me some jewelry, replacements for what had been stolen in a burglary of our home. I refused. I told him it wasn't necessary, that I didn't want any (fool that I was) more jewelry. That must have been what put him in a foul mood.

He went into town with Tanya Robbins, also a house guest there. When they returned, I could see his mood had only gotten worse. Tanya told everyone how he was bombarded by fans wanting his autograph and, knowing the finale was to air that night, they wanted him to tell them how "The Fugitive" ended.

At the party, David was almost antisocial. He had been drinking since midafternoon. He ate very little dinner and seemed as though he really wanted to be someplace else, alone. As the evening progressed, his mood turned even more sullen, insisting that Louise play only Sinatra records, with the volume blasting.

Most of the guests began leaving shortly before midnight. I couldn't help but notice the puzzled way they looked at David. He wasn't even saying goodbye. I was terribly embarrassed and was making excuses for him. We all tried to get him out of this frame of mind, but to no avail. He became verbally abusive and loud. We distanced ourselves from him, hoping he would snap out of it. He sat on the veranda, listening to the Sinatra records and drinking and grumbling to himself.

At around one o'clock, we found him passed out. It was impossible for us to arouse him, so we decided not to try to move him at all. Louise brought pillows to put under and around his head and a blanket to cover him. Louise and Elliot retired, and Tanya and I sat up most of the night talking. She was trying to comfort me, knowing how distressed I was over David's actions.

The next morning, after David had slept it off, he was feeling remorseful and embarrassed over his behavior. At breakfast, knowing that Elliot was returning to New York on business, Tanya was going to Portugal with her mother and he was off to Kenya, David invited Louise to be his guest and join me for a couple of weeks in Cannes, France. That was the first I heard of my impending trip. I didn't really want to go anywhere, but I welcomed the opportunity to have something to do while he would be in Africa.

The next day at the New York airport, with everyone going off in different directions, my farewell with David left me feeling empty. With memories of David's behavior at the party still fresh in my mind, my stomach was in knots. I felt there was something wrong between us, but I didn't know what. How can two people resolve their problems, if one person doesn't know what the problems are?

Louise and I had been in Cannes for several days and I had only heard from David once, letting me know he had arrived safely in Kenya. Louise had to contend with my tears and feelings of confusion over my situation with David.

It was about the sixth day when David called to say his trip had been cut short and he was returning to the States. His plane would be arriving early the next morning in London to catch the connecting flight to New York. I said I would join him there for the time he had between flights.

I didn't have much time to prepare. I spent most of my time on the phone with foreign operators trying to get a flight in time for his arrival. I arrived late that evening and went directly to my room at the hotel near the airport. I wanted to get some sleep. I was awakened by David's call at around four o'clock in the morning, saying he had arrived earlier than expected and had only about an hour and a half before his next flight.

I was anticipating a romantic interlude, hoping to remove any obstacles that stood in our way. I wanted to greet him at the door but realized the nightgown and robe I had hastily thrown in my bag were hardly appropriate for what I had in mind. Today, I would know better and wrap myself in a large bath towel to greet him. Instead, I quickly dressed in my Pucci dress (which was the rage at the time), in which I knew my figure looked great. I really was hoping David would see me as he used to.

We embraced at the door. I detected a look of surprise and disappointment in his eyes, finding me fully clothed. We went to find a coffee shop, but ended up having coffee from a vending machine. We chatted as though we were strangers. It was so awkward and distressing. Shortly after, he left for his flight back to New York. I reluctantly returned to finish my trip with Louise, fighting my emotions. How much I wanted to be on that plane with him. David was in New York and, I learned later, had made plans to see Michele and Jimmy there. Again, I felt left out of his life.

The office of Fred Barman, David's business manager, was directly across the street from the Sierra Towers. There was an office suite available down the hall there and David decided to take it for his own.

Because David had bagged quite a few animals on his safari, we decided on a jungle theme for the office decor.

I found green, leaf-patterned wallpaper and a throne chair for his desk. I had the chair sandblasted and left it in its natural raw state, then covered the upholstery with green patent leather. His desk was an oblong antique table. We built bookcases against one wall. We allowed spaces on the floor for the lion and zebra skins to be placed. Victor began splitting his time between David's new office and the apartment. In the meantime, life with David was about to get worse.

CHAPTER XII

The script for "The Shoes Of The Fisherman" had arrived from Abby, along with the handsome contract he had negotiated. David was very enthused. He felt this film was his first time in the Class A category. It certainly had an all-star cast: Anthony Quinn, Sir Laurence Oliver and John Gielgud. He was looking forward to it.

Learning we would be spending at least three months in Rome to shoot the film, we took Kathy with us. When we arrived in Rome we rented the villa that Elizabeth Taylor and Richard Burton had recently vacated.

The villa was off the Anulare, the road that circles all of Rome. There was a guardhouse at the bottom of the long winding road that led to the palatial estate. It was approximately ten acres of grounds surrounded by dense woods. The interior was mostly marble, which, combined with the villa's huge rooms, made it very cold and unfriendly. The villa also had an enormous kitchen and a butler's pantry with ample quarters for the help we hired. At one side of the house was a pool and formal gardens surrounding the rest of it. There were elaborate antiques. The villa had several bedrooms on the second floor, which was good, because we had invited some guests from the States. It was not the cozy atmosphere we were accustomed to, but it served its purpose.

We settled in. Kathy and I would explore the ruins and other sights of Rome while David was working. We were provided a car and driver for our stay in Rome. "The Shoes Of The Fisherman" was being filmed at the Cinecittá Studios. The car would take David to work, then return to the villa for my use when I needed it.

David arrived home late from work on several occasions, but I made no mention of it. Ralph Stolkin's daughter Nancy, was in Rome at that time and contacted us. She invited Kathy to join her on a side trip to Portugal. It was then, on the help's day off, that I was alone in the villa without a car. It was dark and creepy. All I could hear were dogs howling in the distance.

I was scared. I called the studio to find out how soon David would be home. They told me they had "wrapped" for the day several hours before. I sat there in the dark, empty house and felt like I was in the middle of a horror movie. On top of that, my thyroid was still giving me problems.

After waiting, becoming more and more frightened in that huge mausoleum, I called George England, the producer. He told me he had not seen David since the end of the day's shooting. I don't speak Italian and it was difficult getting a taxi, but I managed to get one. I went to the studio to see if I could find him, but they gave me no clue as to where he might be.

I returned to the villa to wait some more in this desolate place. I was in the front room when he finally arrived. My patience worn thin, I screamed at him;

"DAVID, WHERE THE HELL HAVE YOU BEEN? ... THEY TOLD ME YOU LEFT THE STUDIO HOURS AGO ... YOU KNOW I'M SICK AND I WAS REALLY WORRIED!" I shouted.

"YOU HAVE ALL THE TIME IN THE WORLD FOR YOURSELF ... I NEED A LITTLE DIVERSION, TOO. I NEED SOMETHING TO HELP ME UNWIND AFTER SHOOTING ... A BUNCH OF US GO OUT FOR A FEW DRINKS ...," he yelled.

"BUT ... WHAT ABOUT ME? ... DID IT EVER OCCUR TO YOU THAT I MIGHT NEED YOU HERE ... WITH ME ... INSTEAD OF BEING LEFT ALL ALONE? ... HOW COULD YOU BE SO INCONSIDERATE?" I ranted on.

At this point, we were both raising our voices, at which time I shouted;

"I HATE YOU!"

"YOU HATE ME?" he exclaimed.

Those words must have taken a toll on David. I never got to explain my meaning.

It is amazing how close love and hate can be. Here was the man I truly adored, and yet, at the same time, I hated him. I left the room silently, my emotions drained. There was comfort in the fact that he was home. Nothing more was said about this matter when I awoke the next morning. We went on with our lives as if nothing happened.

Michele Lee and Jimmy Farentino visited us shortly after this terrible argument. I tried to make everything appear normal. We explored Rome together, with Michele's camera clicking away, saving fond memories, for posterity. They spent about a week with us, which we thoroughly enjoyed. A couple of days before Michele and Jimmy were to continue on their journey, Dani and Buddy Greco arrived. The six of us would go to the favorite little sidewalk cafes that David and I had discovered, and the cook made some wonderful dinners at home.

When Michele and Jimmy left, Dani and Buddy were going on to Greece. David had a few days off from filming, so we decided to join them. We had to get a driver in Athens, because none of us could read their road signs.

In Greece, I had developed terrible cramps in my legs and feet. I thought it may be part of my thyroid condition. My medication was not working. It was a good thing we didn't plan on a long stay, because we would have had to head back anyway.

I went into a hypothyroid state where I could barely lift my toothbrush, or a cup to my lips. I made arrangements to return to L. A. alone, to find a doctor who could help me since I could not communicate with the doctors in Rome.

My plane arrived late in the evening. I called Frank Liberman. He came to my rescue by recommending a Dr. Sternstein, who came to my home at about eleven o'clock that night. Had I not left the door unlocked, he would not have been able to get in because I was to weak to get up. He checked me over, gave me a injection to help me sleep. He told me he would contact Dr. Perzig, a specialist in this field and arrange an appointment the next day.

A date was set to have my thyroid removed on the first of July.

After my medication was changed, and I was feeling a bit more like myself, I was able to return to Rome to be with David until he completed the film.

The production over, we returned home. The script for "Where It's At" was waiting for David. It was to be filmed at Caesar's Palace in Las Vegas, and David was needed there to start production the last part of June. That meant I would have to go through my pending surgery alone, because it was scheduled for the first of July.

"Where It's At" was to be filmed in the "Frank Sinatra Suite" and casino at Caesar's Palace Hotel in Las Vegas. It starred David Janssen and Robert Drivas, with Rosemary Forsythe and Brenda Vaccaro as the female leads.

David had been in Las Vegas about a week and I joined him immediately after my release from the hospital, with bandages on my neck. I was still weak from the surgery. David showed less consideration for my condition than ever. He had no tolerance for illness, whether his or anyone else's.

During the first three or four days, I stayed in our suite waiting for David to return after each day's filming. He spent little time with me. He would come in after work, freshen up and then go down to the casino. I would have room service alone, quite frequently. He spoke admirably about Anthea Silbert, the wardrobe designer. My suspicions began gnawing at me again.

As soon as I was able, I would go down to the set to watch the filming. Because of David's waning attention, I felt more and more that he was carrying on with someone but couldn't detect who it was. I felt so alone, I wasn't in touch with any of my old friends in Las Vegas, I wasn't up to that. I wasn't about to let anyone notice our differences.

Brenda Vaccaro's mother was staying with her and I would join them for lunch or breaks in the filming. My uneasiness never left me. I felt that everyone on the set must know what I didn't know.

One night he took me to a casino out of the hotel, trying to lift my spirits and act as if nothing were wrong. He was drinking heavily and started to gamble. He was losing substantially, asking for $1,000 markers one after the other, which the management was all too happy to give him. I felt this was very unfair and brooded about it. I took it upon myself to go to one of the owners to tell him that we were in no position to lose that kind of money and the pit boss had no right to extend that kind of credit to someone as drunk as David obviously was.

He must have taken pity one me, seeing the bandages on my neck, my tearing and bulging eyes, the evident mental state I was in. He said he would pull down the markers. When I told David what I had done he was furious with me. To rectify what I had done, he drew a check the following day and went immediately to pay his debt.

David had recently developed an interest in photography and had purchased a very good camera and lenses. He was snapping away candid shots at the cast and crew. He often spoke highly of Anthea Silbert and negatively, but with equal intensity, about Rosemary Forsythe. I was beginning to suspect he was interested in Anthea. He had some film developed and was showing me the photos. Strangely, there were few of Anthea and other cast members, but many of Rosemary, some even with her hair still in curlers.

One evening when David hadn't come up from work, I gained the courage to go down and confront him. I couldn't tolerate the suspense and anguish building within me. I was still recuperating from surgery, my eyes were still bulging and I felt so ugly. If ever I needed reassurance, it was then.

When I arrived down in the casino, David was sitting at a table in the lounge with a drink in front of him and a bunch of chips in his hand. He was alone. I was angry because he was showing so little regard for what I was going through. It was infuriating that he was practically ignoring me as he continued toying with the chips. In exasperation, I flung my hand under his, sending the green and black chips flying into the air, spilling all over the table and floor.

His face was red, probably from a combination of anger and embarrassment. People were looking at us as he was scurrying to pick up the chips. I stood up and ran back to the suite to have a good cry. When he returned to the room much later, we apologized to each other. David saw the humor in it from the spectators' viewpoint, and we shared a good laugh.

On the surface things appeared to be normal. Instead of trying to win back his love, I was pushing him further and further away. If only I had someone to advise me of what he may have been thinking and feeling, perhaps I could have prevented what was to come. My suspicions of his infidelity kept creeping into my consciousness. I was still hoping that our love was strong enough to survive this crisis.

CHAPTER XIII

When filming was over and we returned to L. A., I felt somewhat more secure in the familiar surroundings of our home. It was approaching August 23, 1968. We were going through the motions of leading a normal married life. David was up early to go to his office and prepare for a meeting with Abby and some studio executives.

After he left, I allowed negative thoughts to enter my mind as I recalled the time two years before when I had to go into Cedars to have polyps removed from my vocal cords. Then, I had been scheduled to be hospitalized two days.

David and Frank Liberman drove me to the hospital in the Rolls Royce the night before my surgery. David kissed me goodbye and said he would visit me in the afternoon following the operation.

My daughter Kathy came to see me that following morning. I was out of recovery and back in my room. My doctor came in right after Kathy. He examined me and was so proud of his work, he said there was no reason for me to stay in the hospital another day, that I probably would be more comfortable at home. He said I should not try to speak for one week before he reexamined me in his office. I was released from the hospital. Cedars provided me with a large thick writing pad and felt-tip pen to communicate with. Kathy drove me home.

As we entered the driveway I noticed the Rolls was not in the garage,
only the station wagon and David's Lamborghini. I thought that was
bizarre because David never drove the Rolls without me. My first
thought was that he had not returned home at all since leaving me at
the hospital. The monster Jealousy was rearing its ugly head again.

Once inside the house, I wrote for Kathy to call David's office. They
had no idea where he was. I scribbled; "Frank Liberman." She called
him, he had not seen or heard from David since leaving me at the
hospital.

The telephone rang. Kathy answered. It was Ralph Stolkin calling
from New York to invite us to a charity ball in November at the
Waldorf-Astoria. I quickly wrote a note for Kathy to advise him that we
(Kathy and I) were on our way to New York, would he arrange accommodations for us at the Carlyle Hotel. He told Kathy we would be his
guests. He had year-round residence in the Carlyle's penthouse.

Of course, Ralph had no idea of the turmoil I was in. Then I
instructed Kathy to call the airlines and book us on the next flight to
New York: I did not want to be home when David returned. Kathy made
our reservations with TWA and we only had about four hours in which
to be at the airport.

I wrote for her to call Beatrice to rush over and help me pack. She
arrived within a half hour of Kathy's call and packed two small bags
for me while Kathy attended to her own packing. I asked her to take
care of Diane, that we had to go to New York and would return soon.
When she asked where "Mr. J" was, I told her I did not know.

Kathy and I made it to the airport on time. I was miserable during
the entire flight. I was not supposed to smoke after the surgery, but I
did.

It was nearly midnight when Ralph's limousine met us at the airport
and drove us to the hotel. It was good to see Ralph, but I couldn't tell
him why I made this unexpected trip. Kathy explained about my
surgery.

The next morning I asked Kathy to visit her father. I really just
wanted to be alone. I needed the solitude to sort things out. I was
certain David was being unfaithful again, and it was eating away
at me.

Obviously, by now David would have learned from Beatrice that we
were in New York and where we could be reached. Yet he had not

called. I wondered if he had even called the hospital. I was in a terrible state, emotionally and physically. I believe now that my doctor was wrong, I should have remained in the hospital for the second day. The stress of my suspicions about David and the physical strain of the trip were just too much for me.

Kathy left immediately after breakfast. Ralph went out for an appointment and the maids finally finished their work. At last I was alone. I was terribly dismayed, trying to understand why David was behaving like this.

Kathy and Ralph both returned early in the afternoon. I hoped they didn't mind if I had dinner in my room. Ralph volunteered to treat Kathy to a Broadway play, so I could be alone and rest.

We had been in New York for two full days and I had not left the suite. Finally, the telephone rang. It was David.

"Ellie, what are you doing in New York? Is anything wrong?" he asked, as if I had no cause for alarm or worry.

I shouldn't have been speaking yet but I did, barely. I told him how hurt I was that he had not visited or even called me in the hospital and that it was apparent he had not been home the night I was in the hospital.

"Where have you been ... with whom? Why haven't you called me before now?" I asked.

He explained that he had spent the night in his dressing room at the studio. That he had been working very hard and, with the time difference, this was the first opportunity he had to call. I accepted his explanation, maybe because I wanted to. My need was to go home and have him hold me in his arms again. I was feeling rather foolish and felt this whole episode was my fault.

I told David we would return the following day. Kathy made our return reservations for the next morning. I felt so relieved and was actually convincing myself that David's explanation was believable.

David met us at the airport. I still could barely talk and was carrying my pad and pen. He understood that I shouldn't be speaking and accepted the fact that I had to write notes. As I now reflect on our drive home, David did appear uneasy at first. He seemed cautious in choosing his words. I think he was probing me to see if there was anything I wasn't telling him. It was good to be home. I drew a "happy face" on my pad and wrote, "I love you!" He smiled and seemed more relaxed.

He seemed happy to have me home, took my pad and drew a "happy face" under mine and wrote under it, "I love you, too!"

It was only a little past five, and he told Beatrice that we did not want dinner. We went into our bedroom and prepared for bed. It felt so good lying in his arms, watching television. I was so exhausted, I fell asleep early.

The next morning I awoke to the aroma of fresh coffee perking in the kitchen and the sound of the shower running in David's bathroom. It was so nice, things were back to normal. It was around six-thirty and he was preparing to go to the studio. The maid brought us a tray with our coffee mugs and thermos, freshly squeezed orange juice, the morning news-paper, and a bud vase with a flower, just picked from the garden or pulled out of the arrangement that was on the dinner table the night before.

David came out of the bathroom, freshly shaved and showered. There he was, in those great-fitting boxer shorts that he had custom-made, and I must say I loved seeing him in them. He had great legs, long and muscular.

He drank his coffee as he dressed. He had a routine to follow. I, on the other hand, lounged with my coffee while listening to the music on the radio. I watched him as he went through his paces of dressing. He usually chose a jump suit or slacks with a sports shirt, long-sleeved but rolled up to the elbows, and o socks under his black velvet moccasins.

After he finished dressing he came over to my side of our bed, as he usually did, sat on the edge and gave me a warm kiss goodbye. As always, he said, "I love you. Talk to you later." He then left for the studio.

I turned off the radio and put the TV on. I poured myself a second cup of coffee and read the newspaper. I felt so much better being back in my own bed. I was secure and promised myself there would be no more fits of jealousy on my part.

The following day was normal. I was still resting from the trip to New York, my operation, and the stress I had been under for the past week. I had started practicing with my voice and could still barely speak but there was no real discomfort or pain. The doctor had told me not to speak more than absolutely necessary.

Now, two years later, this memory was still vivid and I was recalling this episode with a mixture of feelings. One minute I felt apprehensive.

The next minute I was filled with great hope, because we planned to celebrate our tenth wedding anniversary, and I would think about how to make the next ten years the happiest for both of us.

It may appear that during those last few years there was only unhappiness. That was not the case. There were many wonderful times in between, never a day that he and I didn't profess our love for each other.

My deep thoughts were interrupted by the telephone. It was Dani Greco. Dani wanted to arrange an anniversary party for us, a small private gathering in their apartment, with just our most intimate friends. I thanked her and told her I would call David and get back to her. I called David at his office and he said it would be okay, if that's what I wanted. I told him I thought it would be nice and we would be able to go home early.

David, while not sounding overly enthused, was warm to me on the phone. Now I was full of hope for our marriage. The anniversary party was something I was looking forward to, thinking we could start anew.

Over the next week or so, the hours David kept were quite erratic. I did not suspect anything, really, until the night before the party when he didn't come home. David still had his own mobile dressing room. When he was missing, I assumed that he was there.

David came home several hours before we were to go upstairs to the Grecos. I was so happy to see him and was determined to make this anniversary the best we'd had. I didn't question him at all about where he had been.

Most of the guests were already there when we arrived. After exchanging greetings, we were served cocktails. The table was full with a beautiful array of hors d'oeuvres. Dani announced that she had prepared a special dinner. On the buffet was a large cake decorated with "Happy Tenth Anniversary, David and Ellie."

David presented me with two beautiful gifts from Tiffany's Jewelers, a gold watch and a pearl-and-gold bracelet. Then Buddy proposed a toast; some of the guests including Angie Dickinson and Burt Bacharach, Michele Lee and Jimmy Farentino, gathered around to admire the gifts and wish us many more years of happiness.

It was only moments later that David asked me to join him on the balcony. We stood gazing at the lights of the city below, "Like newlyweds," I thought, and I held onto his arm.

Without looking at me and staring out into space, he said:

"Ellie, it's over between us ... I want to be with Rosemary."

I was stunned. It is a good thing I was holding his arm, or I would have collapsed to the floor.

"You have to be joking, David ... you can't mean that ... NOT NOW ... This is our TENTH ANNIVERSARY!" I said, trying to hold back my emotions.

"I don't want to ruin the party, but I have to leave now," he continued.

"David, you can't ... you can't be serious ... we can work this out ... I love YOU ... I love YOU ... and I know you LOVE ME!" I said, tears blurring my eyes.

"I'm sorry. It's what I'm going to do!"

I let go of his arm and I went into the living room and sat down, thinking I could handle myself. I couldn't control the tears and ran from their apartment to the elevator. David followed.

We sat on our sofa. I was pleading with him, I told him that I knew things would be different. David had his mind made up.

He told me not to worry that everything would be all right, that half of everything would be mine, a worry which at the time did not concern me. I couldn't believe he would think that money could possibly ease my pain. David went to our bedroom and packed a few things. A few minutes later he came into the living room and said he'd send for the rest of his things, and left.

After many hours of crying, I fell into a fitful sleep in the early hours of the morning. When Beatrice came in around ten A.M., I awoke to feelings of bewilderment, of emptiness. My eyes were red and swollen. I didn't say anything to Beatrice, I just wanted her to do her work and leave me alone.

A couple of days later when I got my bearings, I called Frank Liberman. I had written out exactly how I felt an announcement should be worded for the press. I had written and rewritten a statement at least a dozen times, trying to make it sound right. I wanted this to appear as a temporary separation. I asked him if he would give Rona Barrett the exclusive, provided she promised to word it exactly as I had written. Assuring him she would, like all tabloid lies, she didn't.

I had secluded myself in the apartment for several weeks, hoping David would come to his senses and return to me. I was literally walking around with a nervous breakdown.

One afternoon David did come home. Beatrice, hearing the key in the door, went to see who was entering. When she asked him what he was doing there, he turned and left. She told me he looked confused. Had I been the one to go to the door instead of Beatrice, things might have turned out differently.

Weeks passed. I continued waiting for David, not rushing to do anything. On November 22, 1968, with a heavy heart, I went to Tiffany's in Beverly Hills to return the watch and bracelet David had given me. They accepted the bracelet but told me he must have purchased the watch someplace else. I just couldn't bear to have them, feeling there was no love in their giving. With the turmoil I was in, I didn't think to return them sooner. I just knew I could never wear them, that they would always be a reminder of the painful moments when he gave them to me.

Eventually, I had to get out of my self-imposed hermit's existence. I had to do something to occupy my mind and decided to open a small antique shop. I found a good location on Robertson Boulevard. I called David and, without mentioning our current situation, told him of the idea and said I would need his financial backing. He told me he would call Fred Barman and I could pick up a check for "whatever you want."

Kathy became my right hand at working the shop. We designed and had stationery printed. I bought a Chevrolet El Camino wagon, and compiled my list of importers and wholesale dealers and auctions. We even took a trip to New York to meet with the top European importers and bought a small amount. For our grand opening, we sent flyers to all the interior decorators and designers. We had a limited, but high-quality inventory.

All through the process of putting this venture together the tears flowed, uncontrollably; it didn't matter where I was or whom I was with, they just came upon me, embarrassing as it was. I was breaking down.

I continued my sessions with Dr. Ruben, though we switched to telephone sessions lasting an hour or two. I learned that David had stopped seeing him completely.

I tried to get back into the social swing. Peggy Burke was a dear friend during this time. She would force me to go out with her to the Polo Lounge and other places, just to try and take my mind off David.

One night, she picked me up and we met Paul at The Factory, a posh, exclusive private club which had been converted from a manufacturing plant. We arrived shortly before Paul. A friend of Paul's, whose name escapes me, came to our table to say hello to Peggy. After being introduced, he asked me to dance. I was politely declining when Peggy urged me on. When we got to the dance floor, my knees buckled, I almost fell to the floor. I could hardly stand. He was patient with me and helped me back to my table. How embarrassing and frightening it was for me.

A bit later, David unexpectedly came in alone. He had been drinking but was reasonably sober. He joined us and was very pleasant to me. It felt so good, like old times. We spent an hour or two enjoying the group we were with, playing pool and having drinks. Peggy suggested we all go to their house and Paul would prepare some of his famous pasta and we could continue playing pool if we chose.

We did. Paul was in the kitchen making the pasta. Peggy, David and I were in their pool room with the rest of the group. Peggy was at the bar fixing us drinks, with David seated on a stool opposite her. Peggy told him that he was a bad influence on Paul, that she thought Paul may be playing around on her.

David responded, "Paul doesn't need any influence from me, he does pretty good with the girls on his own. Has for years,"

With that, as I turned to look in their direction, Peggy slapped David, very hard. Paul was emerging from the kitchen at the same instant and saw it, too.

"Paul, your wife just slapped me!" David said, with a smile on his face.

"Peggy, why did you slap my friend?" Paul said, jokingly.

"Because I told her you don't need my help getting girls," David interjected.

Paul, still thinking it was all a joke, returned to the kitchen for more food and Peggy slapped David again, even harder.

I was astounded at what I was witnessing. I knew Peggy wasn't joking and she was getting angry. The rest of the group stared in silent shock.

"That's for telling Paul what I said!" she told David.

With that David walked over to me, took my arm and said, "Come on, Ellie, we're leaving!"

We didn't even say goodbye. I glanced over my shoulder at Peggy. She understood.

I thought we would have a chance to reconcile our differences that night, but David silently drove me straight home. He left me at the lobby door without even getting out of his car. Several times when we came close to reconciling, fate seemed to step in and spoil our chances.

The apartment seemed so empty without him: it was only hours ago I had such high hopes. It was such a letdown. The way the evening ended, I decided to put everything out of my mind and concentrate on the antique shop. I was determined to wait David out, to give him all the time he needed. I would be there when he was ready to come home.

CHAPTER XIV

I would hear all kinds of reports and read in the tabloids that David's relationship with Rosemary was very volatile, to say the least. That gave me patience to continue waiting. Rumors had it and it appeared in the tabloids that David's drinking was heavier than ever and that he was even drinking on the set, something he never did before.

Rosemary not only kept up with him but actually outdid him in that vice. Reports of their public battles were widespread. Rosemary had a two-and-a-half-year-old daughter, Alexandria, who obviously had won David's heart. Rosemary had brought the baby and nanny with her to the bungalow he had rented for them, at the end of the drive next to the Sierra Towers, where I was living. I was startled that they were living so close and it made me feel that maybe David wasn't completely sure what he wanted to do.

When I learned they were living practically next door, I went to see David one late afternoon. I wanted to try to get some form of commitment from him, what his intentions were. Things had been going on for over ten months and it seemed as though he was happy being married to me as long as he could have Rosemary and Rosemary's baby, too. I wasn't going to sit still for that. The houseman, being the kindly soul he was, told me David was expected shortly and I could wait in the living room.

The dining room table was already set for a romantic candlelight dinner for two, a sight which was wrenching my heart as I waited impatiently.

When David arrived and saw me sitting in his living room, the color drained from his face.

"What are YOU doing here?" he inquired.

"I think it's time ... we should talk!" I stated.

"About what?" he asked.

"About us ... Should I find an attorney? ... Is that what you want me to do? ... I don't want us to end this way ... I don't want us to fight," I said, almost pleading.

"Get a lawyer ... If that's what you want ... Do it .. I'm not going to stop you ... I told you, half is yours!" he murmured, almost condescendingly.

I stood up without a word and left the bungalow. Walking the few steps to the car, my emotions erupted. Tears gushing, I started the engine and in my haste I struck the curved concrete wall, putting an ugly scrape on the right front fender of the Rolls. I don't remember how many hundreds of dollars that scratch cost. What a fiasco this entire visit was.

I returned home. For months now, my close friends had urged me to seek a lawyer's advice. They didn't want to see me end up the "bad guy" and lose anything that was rightfully mine. I had not wanted to think of such a possibility.

Even now, when I heard it from David's own mouth that he didn't care, I wasn't about to act in haste ... or anger ... or out of the hurt I was feeling. I was willing to give it more time. I still had hope he would come back.

Sidney Korshak, who negotiated all the contracts for the Teamsters Union offered to be the go-between for David and myself, to arrange a settlement that would be agreeable to both of us. My well-meaning friends influenced me not to go in that direction. What bad advice that turned out to be.

David and I had gotten together several times during the eighteen months since our splitting up — usually after a knock-down-drag-out fight he had with Rosemary during their stormy relationship.

I remember one such time vividly. We went to Matteo's for dinner and, as we passed Lucille Ball and Gary Morton's table, she exclaimed her delight in seeing us back together again. Lucy and I used to play backgammon at her house quite often and frequently discussed the parallels of our marriages. It was difficult, but we told them that we were just having dinner to talk and get some things ironed out. Lucy looked very disappointed.

We had a pleasant dinner and David remained cold sober. I felt as if he were searching for a macho way of undoing what had been done, of wiping away the hurt. I was very calm and open with him. He didn't make any positive moves, so I resigned myself to more waiting.

Many times he would call me, sometimes very late at night when he was very drunk. He would break down on the phone, even admitting that he hated the position he was in, knowing he had put himself there.

However, after I would tell him he could come back and we would work it all out, he would say that he'd call me later and hang up. Then I wouldn't hear from him for weeks or even months.

By now, it had been a couple of months since I'd have any contact with David. Hope of any reconciliation with him had disappeared and I resigned myself to the fact that a divorce was the only resolution. Painful as the decision was, I knew anything would be better than the way I was living.

I thought maybe, just maybe, if I did file for a divorce, the shock might prompt David to reverse his thinking. I engaged the law firm of Gillen and Scott to file a "Petition for Dissolution of Marriage," new in California family law, and mine was one of the first filed.

After being served the papers, David retaliated by retaining Arthur Crowley, one of the most prominent divorce lawyers in the state. Everyone told me that I would be pulverized, that my attorneys were not in the same league as Mr. Crowley. The best recommendation given me was for Ed Raskin. I dismissed Gillen and Scott and hired Ed Raskin. Due to his ailing health, he asked Sidney Traxler to be his co-counsel in representing me.

Tanya Robbins, who had recently been through a divorce from her husband of over twenty years and knowing the trauma I would face, offered to come from New York and be with me through this ordeal. She stayed with me at the Sierra Towers. She would do her best to keep up my morale during the nightmare called depositions and, later, through the hearings.

It was the lawyers we each hired who ultimately caused our marriage to be irretrievably broken. Once they were involved, David seemed to have no alternative but to follow their lead. It was so unlike him, the things that were being said he knew, both in his mind and in his heart, were totally false and malicious.

David had employed Fred Barman as his business manager before our marriage. I had absolutely no idea what our assets were, or how much money we actually spent per year. During our marriage, when the money started coming in after Abby became his agent, I was given a "household account" and a "clothing allowance" for me. I seldom spent much from the clothing allowance. There were many times that I would give David cash from either of these accounts when he was short.

When the depositions began, I was to find out just how much "we" were worth. I was astonished. David and Rosemary's weekly bills from Jurgenson's, the posh Beverly Hills market for caviar and other imported delicacies, alone would almost have maintained my modest living for a month.

The depositions lasted anywhere from ninety minutes to three hours. Tanya sat patiently in the lawyers' reception room. The depositions were a terrible ordeal for me. I was sitting across the table from the man I loved, our lives being spread out on the table by a bunch of cold, heartless strangers. He would stare down at the table or at a spot on the wall. He wouldn't look at me. Maybe he couldn't. I drew on all my strength to keep my emotions contained. It was a most difficult time.

The depositions were taken and retaken over a several-month period. The lawyers also deposed Abner Greshler, Ralph Stolkin, Fred Barman, Rosemary Forsythe, Victor Gentile, my daughter, Diane, and various bank officers, accountants and retail store managers. The lawyers on both sides were making it a case of financial records, who was entitled to what. Nothing about "love, cherish, honor and obey, till death do us part."

The actual trial began in February of 1970. My heartaches had just begun. Tanya would drive me to the Santa Monica courthouse; I couldn't handle the daily half-hour drive. We had some funny moments with her trying to maneuver the big Rolls Royce Silver Cloud that she affectionately referred to as "The Truck." She was used to driving in Manhattan, and the freeways of Los Angeles amazed her. We said our prayers before leaving the garage of the Sierra Towers each morning and the courthouse parking lot each evening.

David and I would see each other every morning in the courthouse cafeteria where everyone went for coffee. He and his attorneys on one side of the room, us on the other. It was so awkward;we barely spoke, other than exchanging polite "good morning" greetings.

I went through the proceedings in such a mental state, I was really like a zombie. I was there physically, but I didn't focus on any of the words being spoken in the courtroom, except when Rosemary Forsythe was called to the stand.

In all my years with David, the many films and television series he had done, the one world premiere I was genuinely looking forward to was "The Shoes Of The Fisherman." Rosemary Forsythe had stolen that from me. I learned that David had purchased for her to wear on the occasion, a gown from Saks Fifth Avenue costing more than $3,000. In addition, he bought her some very expensive jewelry, shoes and an evening bag.

David had also canceled all my credit cards, on the advice of his lawyers, I'm sure. It was humiliating. Fred Barman, his business manager helped me get them reinstated in my own name.

The dissolution proceedings in open court drew swarms of media. They were reveling in it. I couldn't bear to read the papers each day. At the conclusion of the hearings which lasted over a month, even before the Honorable Judge Wells published his final judgement, many of the tabloids had bold headlines:

"JANSSEN'S WIFE GETS $10 MILLION"!

Nothing could be further from the truth! What a laugh. What a pity.

Appendix I on pages 133–144 are reproductions of the original Court papers, including David's income during our marriage, our community assets and other interesting documents never before published.

Our marriage dissolved, with a stroke of the judge's pen on August 27, 1970, four days after the day we should have celebrated our twelfth wedding anniversary, and I was to face life alone. I had to accept the fact that David would never be walking through the door saying "I LOVE YOU." I thought he was out of my life forever.

It was late in 1972 that David stopped paying my alimony, which was $3,750 per month. Several months passed and I decided that something must be terribly wrong. It was not like David to shirk his responsibilities to anyone or for any reason. I was able to contact him through David Capell, his new business manager. When I questioned him about my alimony, Mr. Capell said I would have to speak directly to David.

Finally, after a few days David called me. He said he didn't have the money. "What a laugh," I thought to myself. He was very short with me. He told me he was having "all kinds of problems."

I had already sold some of the property I received from our settlement, including the Huffington Oil stock and my shares of Huntley House Hotel in Santa Monica, in order to pay the Internal Revenue Service over $102,000; the I.R.S. contended this amount was my share of our community property owed for 1969, when he was squandering money on Rosemary Forsythe. Even though the court had ordered that I be held harmless, Judge Wells' choice of words in his decision, still favored David, and the I.R.S. came after me like a vicious attack dog.

Sidney Lockitch, my tax accountant, did everything he could to help me through this time. He referred me to Bruce Hochman, purported to be the best Certified Public Accountant in the federal tax laws in Beverly Hills at that time. After several weeks of trying to clear the matter, he told me I had to bite the bullet, he saw no way around it.

This left me strapped for funds myself. If it weren't for my share of the out-of-court settlement from a Dino de Laurentis lawsuit, I wouldn't have had money to live on. While we were still married, David had a contract with the famed director-producer Dino de Laurentis to star in a movie to be made in Europe. The movie deal fell through and, at Abby's insistence, David sued the company for breach of contract. The out-of-court settlement was approximately $110,000, of which half was turned over to me as part of the dissolution agreement.

I didn't want to cause David any trouble. I knew things were not going smoothly in his relationship with Rosemary because the tabloids were full of stories. The rumors around the restaurant circuit were that she had become a falling-down drunk. As far as I knew, they were still living together.

David's attitude toward me on the telephone hurt, but more than that, it made me angry. He had worked pretty steadily so he couldn't be financially impaired unless he had been squandering his money very foolishly.

I went to the famed barrister, Marvin M. Mitchelson. I wanted the money David owed me, and I was willing to fight for it.

CHAPTER XV

Mr. Mitchelson told me that he would move the court to force David to pay all back support, with interest. I had great confidence in him. He filed papers with the Court seeking to force David to pay the delinquent alimony. Mr. Mitchelson was very sympathetic to me. He appeared to garner up the temper of a raging bull towards David and his attorney, Arthur Crowley.

With depositions and motions by the lawyers on both sides, and continuances, the matter dragged through the court for about a year. Again, more anxiety and tension.

At last, December 13, 1973, David was found to be in Contempt of Court and was ordered to pay $45,625, or face going to jail for another Contempt of Court.

> **(David) Janssen,** who played the title role in "The Fugitive" on television, was found in contempt of court in Los Angeles and ordered to pay $45,625 in back alimony to his former wife, Ellie.

No victory for me, considering what it cost me. The terms of our Dissolution of Marriage had stipulated that my alimony be paid until I remarried or until I died. Now, Judge Wells, who had retained jurisdiction in this latest action, reduced my alimony from $3,750 per month to $2,200 per month, and set a cutoff date of six years later. This was a result of Arthur Crowley's claiming David was not earning sufficient income to pay such an exorbitant amount. Judge Wells must have been a great fan of David's, because he had favored him in our original dissolution, over the strong evidence supporting my position and vigorous objections by my attorneys.

We didn't know, but found out later, that contracts were being held up for David until this hearing was over. Marvin Mitchelson neglected to find out what David's real assets and deferred income were. I had moved from the Sierra Towers to a flat in Beverly Hills at half the rent to reduce my expenses and Crowley pointed this out to the Judge. Instead of Mitchelson showing the court that, with inflation and rising taxes, I needed more money, he ended up costing me money.

Crowley also brought to the Court's attention that I was an interior decorator, because I had tried my hand at decorating some friends' homes, Michele Lee and Jimmy Farentino's, for one, and that I was capable of earning my own way. That was not the case, because the decorating jobs I was able to get were intermittent and did not provide the income I needed.

Again, Arthur Crowley was widening the bridge between David and myself.

It was soon after the hearing was over that I learned of David's next project, which had been negotiated months before.

The $45,625, which David paid, did get me on my feet.

I went on to open a commodities business and took my good friends, Kay Donno and Patti Hartland, in with me. The commodities business, which was flourishing at that time with novices and "flakes," made us millionaires every night but paupers every morning, because most of our deals failed to materialize. We closed the business several months later. I didn't lose any money, but I didn't make any either.

Meanwhile, David was escorting different ladies about town while I was accepting occasional dates. Carol Conners came into David's life at one point. It was at PIPS, a private club I had joined, that Carol introduced herself. She told me of her love affair with David, that it wasn't going in the direction she wanted. They were spending a great deal of time together writing songs. She asked my advice how to win him over.

"I don't think I'm the right one to ask, since I wasn't able to hold on to him!" I replied.

Carol Conners and David Janssen wrote the lyrics to "My Sensitive, Passionate Man," the theme song for the NBC Movie Premiere of the same name by the Factor/Newland Production Co. in 1977. David was the star, with Angie Dickinson his costar. In the movie, he played an alcoholic, whose life closely resembled his own. A copy of the sheet music can be found on pages 120–121.

Carol might have been the best thing for him, but how would he have known? He was already going full speed ahead towards self-destruction.

I have spoken to Carol in recent years and have come to admire her. She is a genuinely sweet person as well as being very talented.

David and Angie had been an item during the filming of "A Sensitive, Passionate Man." Angie has been quoted in rating her lovers:

"DAVID JANSSEN ... he was the greatest ... Men loved
him. Women loved him. He was the greatest."

There were rumors that David and Dani Greco were steadily dating. I was to learn much later from Buddy Greco how that came about. Just before Buddy's closing night performance in Las Vegas, Dani called Buddy from their home in L. A. and told him not to bother coming home, that she was "going off with David." What a devastating blow. Buddy still had his final show to perform.

Buddy told me recently that he could not believe it. He said that they had been happily married for eleven years, at least he had thought so. In addition, he always thought David was a real friend. According to Buddy, Dani made their divorce nasty and nearly ruined him financially. However, Buddy survived and his career continued on the upswing.

Dani and I had not been friendly since David left me. During our first round of open court hearings, she would appear at the Santa Monica courthouse to have lunch with David, and I could detect the coldness in her looks. Apparently she had her designs on David then, but Rosemary was in her way.

The marriage of David and Dani was publicized widely and was set for October 4, 1975. David was filming his new television series, "Harry O." It was reported that he had asked his good friend, attorney Sidney Korshak, to be his best man. It was also reported that this was Dani's third marriage.

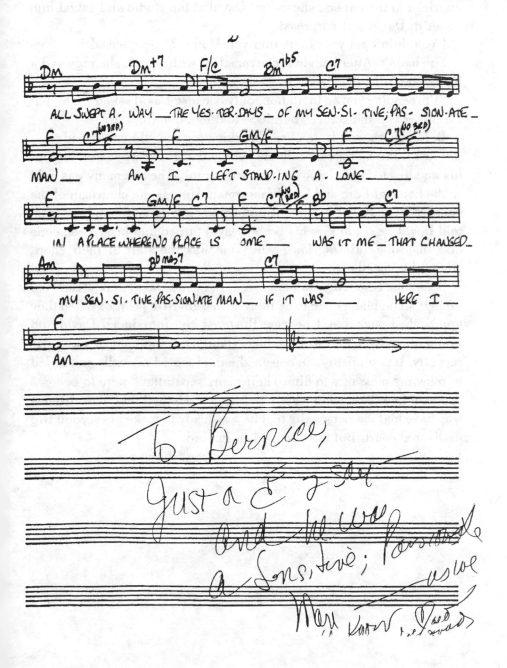

ALL SWEPT A-WAY __ THE YES-TER-DAYS __ OF MY SEN-SI-TIVE; PAS-SION-ATE __

MAN __ AM I __ LEFT STAND-ING A-LONE __

IN A PLACE WHERE NO PLACE IS SOME __ WAS IT ME __ THAT CHANGED __

MY SEN-SI-TIVE, PAS-SION-ATE MAN __ IF IT WAS __ HERE I __

AM __

David's mother related to me recently that when she read about the marriage in the papers, she called David at the studio and asked him about it. David was surprised.

"You didn't get your invitation yet, Mother?" he queried.

She hadn't. After her short conversation with David, she received a telephone call from Dani.

"I'm sending you an invitation, only because David asked me to, but I'd prefer you not come," Berniece told me, quoting Dani.

Berniece, though it was heartbreaking for her, did not attend.

I heard through a very reliable source that David appeared late for his wedding to Dani Greco and was very drunk. The ceremony was held in the home of Edie and Lew Wasserman. He was the chairman of the board of MCA. At the end of the nuptials, when Judge William Rosenthal told David he could kiss his bride, David turned and kissed someone else instead of kissing his bride. That was the start of their short, stormy life together.

Sometime before they were married, Dani and David were at the Polo Lounge when I happened to be there with a group of people. When they approached our table, I became flustered and introduced David and unintentionally failed to introduce Dani. This was told to me fairly recently. It is probably the reason she intercepted my calls and failed to relay my messages to him. Their many separations were to become common knowledge and widely publicized. He had told close friends who have told me personally that he was ready to make his second trip to divorce court. But fate stepped in instead.

CHAPTER XVI

Iam an early riser, usually around seven. This particular morning, I was startled awake by the telephone. It was my friend, Patti Hartland. She was speaking fast, excitedly:

"David's dead ... Turn on the news!" Then, without another word, she hung up.

I sat upright and fumbled for the television remote control. I kept switching channels, trying to find the local news. I was dumbfounded by Patti's call. I was in shock. Surely, she could not have been talking about David Janssen. Not my David! He was only forty-eight years old. He would have been forty-nine on March 27 1980, a little more than a month later.

The next local news came at six-thirty A.M. I had the television in my bedroom on, the TV in the living room on a different channel, and the radios blaring on different stations. I had prepared my coffee as I anxiously awaited the news broadcasts.

On Channel 4, NBC in Los Angeles, his death was the lead story:

David Janssen, the tough-talking TV private eye of "Rich-ard Diamond" and "Harry O" and the falsely-accused hero of "The Fugitive," died today at age 48. Janssen was pronounced dead at Santa Monica Hospital after suffering an apparent heart attack at his Malibu home, said Jerry Pam, a spokesman for the actor. Actor Stuart Whitman, an old friend, said he was driving by Janssen's home at about four-thirty A.M. when he saw a paramedic's ambulance and a fire truck. Whitman said he went inside and saw the paramedics at work trying to restore Janssen's heartbeat.

They had taken him out of bed and they were working on him. It must have been half an hour altogether. One of them said, "I think I've got a heartbeat," and they took him to the hospital.

Janssen, born David Meyer on March 27, 1931 in Naponee, Nebraska, was a success in nearly every television role he tried, starting with the "Richard Diamond" series in 1957 and extending through to "Harry O" in the midseventies. But most successful was "The Fugitive" series from 1963 to 1967 in which Janssen played Dr. Richard Kimble, a man falsely accused of murdering his wife and endlessly seeking the elusive one-armed man who actually did the job. Other shows included "The Naked City," "Checkmate," "Follow the Sun" and "O'Hara, U.S. Treasury."

Whitman said he took Janssen's wife, Dani, to the hospital and were met by the doctor and a chaplain.

"He was really quite young," Whitman said. "He started a new movie called 'Father Damien' just two days ago."

Janssen was playing the title role, a leper colony priest.

"We're all going to miss him. He was one hell of a good friend. He was a professional, through and through, and I'm sure there are a lot of his fans who also feel a deep loss," Whitman added.

I dropped my cup on the kitchen floor, stumbled to a chair and sat down. I was trembling and sobbing uncontrollably, when the telephone rang again. It was Kay Donno. She realized I could not talk and said she would come right over.

I could not believe the news. How could this happen to David?

He was so young and such a strong man. I was in a daze. I fixed a cup of coffee and lit a cigarette to calm my nerves. I went to my bedroom. I called my daughter Diane, who lived in Las Vegas. I awoke her with the news. She was devastated and broke down. She said she would have to call me later. I then called my daughter Kathy, in Oregon. She too, was shocked. I then tried to reach David's mother Berniece and his sisters Teri and Jill, to no avail. Also Abby Greshler and Frank Liberman, I but couldn't seem to reach any of them.

I kept turning the television channels, trying to learn more. I was chain smoking and drinking cup after cup of coffee. I felt as though I were on the verge of breaking down and I knew I would have to get hold of myself to regain my composure. I just could not believe that the man I still loved had been taken so soon and so young. My heart was laden with grief. I sprawled on my bed sobbing. I couldn't stop. I just couldn't believe it.

Soon, another report on television.

It was basically a repeat of what had been said, with some quotes from Abby.

"David had no history whatsoever of heart problems and his doctor is in just as much a state of shock as we are."

Producer Jean Moore Edwards said Janssen had started work on a television film, "Father Damien," about a leper priest in Hawaii only two days earlier.

"He had put in a full and productive day and was in high spirits when he left the set yesterday," she said in a statement.

Janssen is survived by his wife, Dani. An earlier marriage to Ellie Graham ended in divorce after twelve years. Funeral plans are pending.

When Kay arrived, I was a total mess. Kay made another pot of coffee. When I came out from my shower, we had fresh coffee. I still couldn't stop crying. My telephone began to ring and ring. Kay screened the calls for me. So many old friends were calling to express their condolences, almost as if I were David's widow.

I was trying to find out news of where and when the services would be, but no one knew much of anything at that time. Abby returned my earlier message and told me he would find out and call me back. Kay prepared lunch for us, which of course I couldn't eat. My stomach was in knots.

Frantically, I tried to find out where David would be, where I could go to see him. I knew that Dani would not want me there but I didn't care. He had been my husband for twelve years. No one could keep me from going.

Diane flew in from Las Vegas to help comfort me through this trying time. She stayed with me that night. I awoke early the next morning. The newspaper had just been delivered and Diane prepared coffee and orange juice. There was a large article and photo of David on the front page of the Metro News section of the *Los Angeles Times*. The article said funeral plans were incomplete. The reality of his loss was hitting me hard. I took a sedative.

When I came from my bath there were a pile of telephone messages from all over the country, friends who had known David and me when we were happily married. I just glanced through them, I wasn't in the frame of mind to return phone calls. I did return a call to Tanya Robbins, my dear friend in New York who had supported me through the divorce proceedings.

I was anxiously awaiting the TV news reports, hoping to learn where David would be for visitation. The news finally came in a call from Abby Greshler. He told me the services would be private, no visitation. He said Dani would have to clear all wishing to attend the services.

I was crushed, but I would not allow her to keep me away. The noon news was more repetition of the circumstances surrounding his death, nothing about services. The evening news would announce that a funeral would be held for family and close friends.

There would be no visitation, the announcer reported. Then another blow: The services would be held at ten o'clock on February 17. My birthday. Every year thereafter, I am reminded of this sadness.

There would be many hours of private pain to endure before the scheduled services. Although Diane was there doing everything possible for me, I really wanted to be alone in my grief. I stayed in my bedroom. Diane fielded the continuous ringing of the telephone calls.

Why did he have to die? WHY?

Victor Gentile, David's secretary and aide of many years, called. So did Nicky Blair, another close friend who had attended the Universal Studios acting school with David and was now a successful restaurateur. So many other friends were calling to express their shock and sorrow. It sparked so many memories and I prayed for strength to get through this ordeal. The newspapers carried more stories of the known details of his death. They were raising more questions than providing answers. Actually, there were suspicions being voiced by reporters as to the real cause of his death. One question they posed: Had Fire-Rescue been called in time, could he have been saved?

Diane and I were up very early on Sunday, February 17. We took our turns in the bathroom and dressed by seven-thirty. I chose a black wool suit I had designed and made myself. I thought it ironic I had never worn that suit before. I've never worn it since.

We sat at the dining table having our coffee. My eyes were almost swollen shut. My makeup would not hold, I knew that, but it didn't really matter on this day. Peggy and Kay picked us up and drove us to the Hillside Memorial Park chapel for the services. We arrived at about nine o'clock. A large crowd of curious on lookers were held behind police barricades. David had so many, many fans.

We sat in the car for several minutes. Berniece, Jill and Teri arrived. We left our car and followed a few steps behind them to the chapel door. I put my arm around Berniece. Neither of us could find words. I nodded at Teri and Jill. At the door, a security guard stopped us and was not going to admit us until Abby intervened, and we were ushered in.

I watched as Berniece, escorted by Teri and Jill, went to David's coffin. It was closed, a deep mahogany, covered with white gardenias. It was painful to see Berniece saying goodbye to her only son. She was then escorted to the back of the chapel and seated with Teri and Jill on either side, in front of Diane, Peggy, Kay and me. A few minutes later, Abby came back and escorted Berniece to the front to be seated in the family pew across the aisle from Dani and her close friend Linda Evans.

The chapel was already filling up. Ruth and Milton Berle, Gregory Peck, Johnny Carson, James Garner, George Peppard, Danny Thomas, Jack Klugman, Richard Harris, Robert Stack, Vince Edwards, George Hamilton, Buddy Hackett, Gene Kelly, Paul Burke, Nancy and Tina Sinatra, George Segal, Jack Warden, Anthony Zerbe, Quinn Martin, Barbara and Jackie Cooper, Richard Lang, Michele Lee and James Farentino, Stuart Whitman, Robert Wagner, Rod Stewart. Some of the other women in his life, Suzanne Pleshette, Angie Dickinson, were reported to be there.

The chapel was filled to capacity. Outside, under the hot sun, were hundreds of loyal fans many wiping their eyes. I was very uncomfortable in my wool suit. The weather was unusually warm for this time of the year.

I sat through the services, about an hour and a half, hearing the eulogies by Suzanne Pleshette and others. As we filed out of the chapel, Diane who was there to support me, was walking behind me. She stumbled and almost fainted. Peggy Burke caught her and pushed us outside so she could get fresh air.

The walk up to the mausoleum was long. There were no ushers or guides directing the winding throng of mourners up the hill to the crypt. I was concerned as I watched so many people trampling on the graves of others. As all gathered to watch the final ceremony, the sky turned dark and ominous, as if the angels were sharing our collective grief. I thought it ironic that David was placed in a crypt below a famous producer who had once told him he would never make it as an actor. Poetic justice.

As we were leaving the crypt, the news photographers were snapping photos of everyone. They rushed at me and I pleaded with them not to take any photos of me. They ignored my pleas and snapped away, the flashes almost blinding me.

I was incensed when I read in the papers the next day that I had "sailed in from London for the funeral," when, in fact, I had been living in L. A. for years and had not been abroad except for a long-ago vacation.

Kay, Diane, Peggy and I were all choking back our emotions. Peggy suggested we needed a drink; Kay drove us to the Polo Lounge. I think that gathering helped me more than anything during the past three days. We had a light lunch, and we all reminisced about the good times and what a great guy David really was. We left around five o'clock in the afternoon.

CHAPTER XVII

T hen, alone in my apartment, I faced the finality of death. Having said farewell to the only man I ever truly loved, I was left with memories. Memories that have kept my love alive, a love that will not die.

As I sat alone, some of the words from the television and radio reports and the newspaper accounts of his death flashed in my mind. And so did several burning questions:

"Why did it happen?"

"How did it really happen?"

"Why did the paramedics have to climb a six-foot-high wall to get in?"

"Could the rumors about drugs be true?"

Even now, I'm still searching for the truth. Perhaps someone will come forth who knows it and can answer many of these questions.

In preparing this book, I have relied upon memories, factual information, and details — many of which are included in this book — plus recollections of family and close friends. I do not put much credence in hearsay or secondhand information. However, I do relate on these pages some of the hearsay, which I find questionable, but possibly truthful.

I went to Los Angeles and met with many of our friends, people who had remained friendly with both of us after our divorce. They provided me with information I consider to be extremely reliable and truthful.

I was told by David's chauffeur, Elliott Shapiro, that when he arrived to take David to the studio that morning, Dani opened the door and said words to the effect:

"You won't be needed anymore ... David died this morning" and she then closed the door in his face. He said she was all made up as if she were going shopping.

She reportedly did go shopping. I was told she and Linda Evans went shopping on Rodeo Drive in Beverly Hills and did buy a white silk blouse to wear to David's funeral.

A person very close to them told me that she saw Dani Janssen at around ten o'clock the evening before David's death, and that Dani had prepared a dinner to take to the Malibu home to surprise David.

Dani was living in their Century City condominium and David was living at their Malibu home. Was a divorce imminent? Did they argue that night?

I was horrified when told by a very close friend that she had personally observed David partake of cocaine at a Palm Springs party. She did not know if it was recreational or if he had a habit.

Other reports published in the tabloids said that David had sexual relations with a famous actor's wife in the late afternoon before his death, plus a former Playboy Bunny and a Hollywood party girl the night before he died. This report I know has to be false because it has been substantiated that David worked the two full days prior to his death on the television movie "Father Damien" which had just started production.

David's mother retained attorney Marvin Mitchelson to contest what was purported to be David's Last Will and Testament, prepared in 1977, as filed by Dani Janssen for probate.

From my personal knowledge, David was very kind, and always generous, almost to a fault. During our marriage, he helped his mother financially, and even helped in the support of my mother. The Last Will and Testament as filed in probate, left nothing to his mother, his sisters, or to our daughters, not to mention those who had served him faithfully for many years, people I know he loved and truly cared for.

As mentioned, David would never have made it in the business world. He turned everything over to people he thought more qualified or that he thought were trustworthy. I have known David to sign documents put before him by those he trusted, without reading them first or asking any questions. In matters handled by his agent, business manager, his accountants and personal secretaries, he was well served by people with high integrity. As to his Last Will and Testament, was it drawn to reflect his last wishes and instructions? Did he even read it? Was he drunk when he signed it?

Paul Ziffren was David's lawyer. His son Kenneth Ziffren, also an attorney in the office, prepared David's Last Will and Testament. As the document indicates, Dani got it all.

Diane had seen David in Las Vegas where she was living at the time. He had come there with Ruth and Milton Berle for a celebrity tennis tournament and invited Diane to join them for dinner. When she arrived at Caesar's Palace, she was escorted to David's table.

"He asked about you," she told me, "and wanted to know how you were feeling.

"The Berles arrived, asked about you, too and seemed so pleased to see me," she continued.

"When we finished dinner, I looked toward David to thank him, he appeared annoyed. The blood seemed to drain from his face. I looked to where he was staring and Dani was walking toward our table. He had several drinks by this time, but seemed reasonably sober. Earlier, he told me he and Dani were having problems. She must not have recognized me, because as she approached the table she created a big scene, screaming at David and cursing.

"I could see that Ruth and Milton were embarrassed. David kept calm. Looking down at the table, he told her, almost in a whisper, to keep her voice down. She got even louder. Everyone in the room was staring at us, especially at her.

"David stood up, took my arm and said, 'Come on honey, let's get out of here.' He apologized to Ruth and Milton as we rushed toward the door, leaving Dani standing there ranting and raving. He said she was supposed to be in L. A. and he didn't even know she was coming to Las Vegas.

"As we were walking to the parking lot, he told me, 'I'm going to leave that bitch. I can't stand it anymore. She's driving me crazy!' "

"Then he kissed me on the forehead," Diane went on. "He said, 'Honey don't worry, you and Kathy are in my Will, you'll be okay. See you later.' Curiously, that happened about a month before he died. Did he have a premonition?"

Appendix II on pages 145–147 show a true and correct copy of David's Last Will and Testament.

After our marriage was dissolved, it hurt me to see David going downhill so fast. I tried my darnedest to slow him down while we were together, but David was a man of many excesses.

We all have our demons. Unfortunately, David's was the bottle. It doesn't matter who you are or what your station in life, drowning yourself in alcohol is a shame.

Our marriage was loving and strong. We struggled together during our first years. I had the best years of his life, and he had mine. As he reached the status of stardom he enjoyed in 1968, our tenth year as husband and wife, the stardom, combined with his drinking, led him to succumb to the other temptations of Hollywood. Perhaps, had I "looked the other way," as many Hollywood wives do, things might have been different.

Had the opportunities for reconciling presented themselves at a time when we both could have recognized what they were, might David still be with us today?

Upon looking back, I find the cliché "time heals all wounds" does apply to me. After those trying times of the breakup and divorce, the hurt and ache have passed, but the emptiness in my life never will.

I wandered. I moved from one coast to the other several times searching for the right place for me. I was fortunate enough to make many friends and meet some very attractive men, but none could fill David's shoes.

Everyone who touches our lives, even in the most minute way, leaves a print which affects our future. As each person comes and goes, we find we are lead on different paths.

I am grateful to all who came into my life, since I have had such a rich and full one.

I count my blessings every day, and I always have.

APPENDIX I
Divorce Settlement

Following is a copy of the Divorce Settlement between Ellie and David Janssen.

RYAN AND TRAXLER

LAW OFFICES

EIGHTH FLOOR UNION BANK BUILDING

9460 WILSHIRE BOULEVARD

BEVERLY HILLS, CALIFORNIA 90212

CRESTVIEW 4-0111

BRADSHAW 2-4404

Attorneys for _____Petitioner_____

SUPERIOR COURT OF THE STATE OF CALIFORNIA
FOR THE COUNTY OF LOS ANGELES

In re the Marriage of:)	
)	No. WE D 14074
Petitioner: ELLIE JANSSEN)	
)	FINDINGS OF FACT AND
and)	
)	CONCLUSIONS OF LAW
Respondent: DAVID H. JANSSEN)	
)	
_____)	

The above action was tried before THE HONORABLE RICHARD L. WELLS, in Department West "G" of the above-entitled Court on FEBRUARY 24, 25, 26 and 27 and MARCH 2, 3, 4, 5, 6, 9, 10, 11, 12, 13, 16, 17, 1970. Petitioner and Respondent appeared in person and through their attorneys; evidence was adduced, the cause was argued orally, in writing and submitted to the Court for decision, and The Court now makes the following FINDINGS OF FACT and CONCLUSIONS OF LAW:

FINDINGS OF FACT

     I.   Petitioner is now, and has been, a bonafide resident of the State of California for more than one year, and of the County of Los Angeles for more than three (3) months immediately preceding the commencement of this action.

     II.   The parties contracted a valid marriage on AUGUST 23, 1958, in Las Vegas, Nevada, and ever since they have been husband and wife.

     III.   The parties separated on AUGUST 23, 1968.

     IV.   There are no children of the marriage.

     V.   Irreconcilable differences have caused an irremediable breakdown of the marriage.

     VI.   The allegations of Paragraph II of the "First Cause of Action for Annulment" in the Respondent's SECOND AMENDED CROSS-COMPLAINT (Annulment or Divorce) are not true.

     VII.   The allegations of Paragraphs 5, 6, 7, 8 and 9 of Petitioner's "ANSWER TO SECOND AMENDED CROSS-COMPLAINT OF DAVID H. JANSSEN FOR ANNULMENT OR DIVORCE" are true.

     VIII.   By stipulation all of the Petitioner's jewelry, furs and clothes are her separate property, and all of Respondent's jewelry and clothes are his separate property.

     IX.   All property of the parties, other than the separate property described in Paragraph VIII above, is Community Property.

     X.   All of the Community Property assets of the parties are listed and valued as follows:

ITEM	VALUE
1. $50,000.00 deferred compensation, or any other sum due to Respondent from Producer's share of a motion picture entitled "MACHO CALLAHAN"	Not valued
2. 7½% interest in T & C PROPERTIES, a Limited Partnership, evidence by a written Agreement of Aug. 1, 1967 in which a general partnership known as "ZIFFREN & ZIFFREN NO. 2" is the general partner, which limited partnership holds real property known as "Town and Country Shopping Center" at 3rd and Fairfax, in Los Angeles, California	Not Valued
3. 10% interest in "HUNTLEY SANTA MONICA" a partnership evidenced by an "Operating Agreement" of June 20, 1968 under which "ZIFFREN & ZIFFREN NO. 2" is "Manager", together with an undivided 10% interest in certain improved real property known as "THE HUNTLEY HOUSE" at 1111 Second Street, Santa Monica, California	Not Valued

ITEM	VALUE

4. 10% interest in L-V PROPERTIES, a partnership evidenced
   by an "Operating Agreement" of June 26, 1968, under
   which "Ziffren and Ziffren No. 2" is "Manager", recorded
   as Document No. 14002 in Book 1519 at Page 614 of
   Recorder's Office in Solano County California, together with
   an undivided 10% interest in certain improved real property
   known as "LARWIN PLAZA SHOPPING CENTER"
   Vallejo, California   Not Valued

5. 14.67% Joint Venture interest in SAHARA SANDS, a
   partnership in which the operating partner is FRED
   BARMAN of 9255 West Sunset Boulevard, Los Angeles,
   California   Not Valued

6. 25% Joint Venture interest in SHADOW PASEO, a
   partnership in which the operating partner is FRED
   BARMAN of 9255 West Sunset Boulevard, Los Angeles,
   California   Not Valued

7. Oil Investment and interest therein, placed with and
   operated by ROY M. HUFFINGTON, INC., of 2210
   Tennessee Bldg. Houston Texas (77002).   Not Valued

8. Cause of action and claim of $250,000.00 against
   DINO de LAURENTIS CINEMATOGRAFICA, S.P.A.,
   and COLUMBIA PICTURES contained in litigation
   on file in NEW YORK SUPREME COURT wherein
   Respondent is Plaintiff   Not Valued

9. Ownership and/or profit sharing interest and all
   interests and rights in and to a television series entitled
   "THE FUGITIVE" derivative from, but not limited to,
   an agreement dated Nov. 13, 1962 between Respondent
   and Q. M. Productions, the producers of said series.   Not Valued

10. "Residuals" due or to come from all motion pictures and
    television, or either, which have been completed to date
    in which Respondent participates   Not Valued

11. Ownership and/or profit sharing interest, and all interests
    and rights in and to a television series entitled
    "RICHARD DIAMOND"   Not Valued

12. Furniture and furnishings formerly in Palm Springs and
    now at Bekins Van & Storage, Beverly Hills, California   Not Valued

13. Cash as of 3/3/70 $83,294.78

14. Furniture in Petitioner's apartment at 9255 Dohency Road,
    Los Angeles, California, known as "Sierra Towers"   8,605.00

ITEM	VALUE
15. Prepaid rent and Security deposit — Sierra Towers Apartment	$1,530.00
16. 1965 ROLLS ROYCE, subject to encumbrance, equity	7,271.80
17. Stock — ELLIE JANSSEN ASSOCIATES, INC. sometimes known as ELLIE JANSSEN INTERIORS	1.00
18. "RAQUET CLUB" Palm Springs Membership and "FACTORY" Membership	1.00
19. OCCIDENTAL LIFE INSURANCE Policy Number 2634840	21.00
20. NORTH AMERICAN LIFE INSURANCE Policy Number L – 574387	1,985.00
21. OCCIDENTAL LIFE INSURANCE Policy Number 4091801	1,000.00
22. Bank Account – ELLIE JANSSEN AND ASSOCIATES, INC.	1,304.32
23. Note of TONI K. HOLT secured by Second Deed of Trust on Palm Springs Property described as Subleasehold estate in and to Lot 3 of Tract 2472 as filed in Book 48, Page 15 Records of Riverside County, California, dated December 12, 1968 in favor of Petitioner and Respondent in the original sum of $12,200.00	10,277.88
24. Receivable from EXCEDRIN contract due to Respondent	58,500.00
25. Stock in DAVID JANSSEN ENTERPRISES, INC. and D.M.J. ENTERPRISES	1.00
26. Stock in ASTRON PRODUCTIONS, a corporation	1.00
27. Stock in LOS ANGELES AIR TAXI SERVICE, INC., a corporation	1.00
28. AFTRA deposit	5.00
29. Equity in Lot #2 of Tract 2928 as shown by Map on file in Book 52, Pages 46 and 47 of Maps, Riverside County, California, subject to First Deed of Trust, and including plans, blueprints and drawings	31,600.
30. Professional equipment in possession of Respondent	5,212.00
31. Prepaid rent, Respondent's office	515.28
32. Furniture, Respondent's office	3,032.08
33. Equities and all interests in 3 parcels of desert land – Palm Desert, Indian Wells and Thermal, subject to encumbrances thereon	1.00
34. Furniture, furnishings and Spencer Orgell Silver in Respondent's residence	10,322.00
35. Piper Aztec Airplane	33,836.20
36. 1969 Rolls Royce, equity	7,734.00
37. 1965 Travel Lodge trailer	18,000.00

ITEM	VALUE
38. Prepaid rent and deposit, Respondent's residence	5,500.00
39. Sovereign Life Insurance Policy #18528	890.00
40. TWA deposit	425.00
41. Tres Vidas Club	5,000.00
42. Tamarisk Country Club	4,800.00
43. All other Club Memberships held by Respondent	1.00
44. Kenya Safari, receivable	1,000.00
45. Los Angeles Air Taxi Service, Inc. account receivable	1,097.00
46. A. Shaw, account receivable	500.00
47. Berrere, account receivable	200.00
48. Pete Wilson, account receivable	206.00
49. Astron Products, account receivable	526.00
TOTAL	$ 305,271.34

XI.   All of the community debts of the parties, other than encumbrances against certain assets which have been taken into account in Paragraph X, are listed and valued as follows:

ITEM	VALUE
1. Los Angeles Air Taxi Service, Inc.	$ 1,106.19
2. Astron Productions	837.50
3. Sahara Sands	2,273.65
4. City National Bank, Beverly Hills – Note	35,000.00
5. All 1969 Income Taxes, State and Federal (whatever the amount)	1.00
6. All 1970 Income Taxes, State and Federal incurred to date, estimated	100,000.00
7. 1967 and 1968 Federal Income tax liability estimated	50,000.00
8. Eli Parker	2,500.00
9. Dr. Naiditch	1,550.00
10. Pension and Welfare, SAG	6,500.00
11. Sovereign Life Insurance, premium notice	335.84
12. City National Bank, interest on note UF-05812	84.97
13. Magla Productions	113.20
14. Carol Hargreaves	143.00
15. Jona Lingerfelder	53.50
16. Pacific Telephone	87.88
17. Top Hat Cleaners	7.85
18. Wilshire Limo. Service	37.80

ITEM	VALUE
19. Huffington Oil charges	$ 19.89
20. Peat, Marwick & Mitchell, additional fees awarded herein	7,350.00
21. Gillen & Scott, attorney fees awarded herein	3,000.00
22. Gillen & Scott, costs awarded herein	98.88
23. Traxler & Raskin, additional attorneys' fees awarded herein	30,000.00
24. Traxler & Raskin, costs awarded herein	405.00
TOTAL	$241,506.15

XII.   The following expenditures made by Respondent constitute a deliberate misappropriation by him to the exclusion of the community property interest of Petitioner, to which Petitioner is entitled to immediate reimbursement of one-half or $17,798.15:

Expenditures in Florida, 1969 (Portion of Exhibit 4–Schedule 2)	$ 2,255.00
Expenditures in New York City, 1968–9 (Portion of Exhibit schedule 3)	4,000.00
General Store (Portion of Exhibit 4, Schedule 6 and Exhibit 46)	1,582.75
Saks Fifth Avenue (Portion of Exhibit 4–Schedule 7)	3,317.35
Jurgenson's (Exhibit 4–Schedule 8)	971.37
Amelia Gray (Portion of Exhibit 4–Schedule 9)	5,147.80
Miscellaneous travel (Portion of Exhibit 4–Schedule 10)	2,100.00
Miscellaneous expenditures (Portion of Exhibit 4–Schedule 11)	2,151.72
Excess rent (Portion of Exhibit 4–Schedule 13)	9,000.00
Alan Austin (Exhibit 14)	163.30
Chequer West (Exhibit 14)	960.75
The Staircase (Exhibit 14)	75.60
Gifts (Exhibit 15)	700.00
Expenditures for Cabrillo residence, servants and food (oral testimony)	$ 3,170.75
TOTAL	$ 35,596.39

XIII.   Respondent paid out $44,200.000 from community funds for gambling losses incurred by him in Las Vegas after August 23, 1968 to the following parties at the time and in the sums indicated, for which the community estate received no valuable consideration:

Caesar's Palace (November 1968)	$ 6,000.00
California Clearing Corporation (November 1968)	6,700.00
The Sands (December 1968)	1,000.00
Danny Schwartz (February 1969)	7,500.00
Caesar's Palace (September 1969)	23,000.00
TOTAL	$ 44,200.00

XIV.   Respondent expended a total of $121,682.61 from community funds after August 23, 1968 (including the $35,596.39 mentioned in Paragraph XII and the $44,200.00 mentioned in Paragraph XIII) all as itemized on Exhibit 4 (schedules 1, 2, 3, 5, 6, 7, 8, 9, 10, 11, 12, 13 thereof), Exhibit 14, Exhibit 15, Exhibit 46 and Exhibit 50 plus the "Expenditures for Cabrillo residence, servants and food" of $3,170.75; however, of these expenditures totalling $121,682.61 only $35,596.39 thereof was a deliberate misappropriation by Respondent and the balance thereof, including the $44,200.00 lost at gambling, was not a deliberate misappropriation.

XV.   Petitioner reasonably requires for her support, in addition to the income she will receive from her share of the community property, and Respondent has the ability to pay, support in the sum of $3,750.00 per month, payable $1875.00 on the 1st and $1875.00 on the 15th of each month commencing MAY 1, 1970 and continuing until the remarriage or death of Petitioner, the death of Respondent, or further order of Court, whichever event first occurs.

XVI.   Petitioner reasonably requires, as and for payment of her attorneys' fees, legal costs and accounting fees reasonably incurred to date of judgment, and in addition to any sums heretofore awarded and paid, the following amounts payable directly by Respondent to the following persons on or before MAY 31, 1970, all of which Respondent has the ability to pay:

Sidney Traxler and Edward M. Raskin	$30,000.00	Fees
Sidney Traxler and Edward M Raskin	405.00	Costs
Gillen & Scott	3,000.00	Fees
Gillen & Scott	98.00	Costs
Peat, Marwick & Mitchell, C.P.A.'s	7,350.00	Fees

XVII.   An equal division of the Community Property can be accomplished by dividing the property as follows and providing payment of debts as hereinafter set forth in Paragraph XVIII:

(1) TO BE EQUALLY DIVIDED IN KIND:

ITEM	VALUE
1. $50,000.00 deferred compensation or any other sum due to Respondent from Producer's share of a motion picture entitled "MACHO CALLAHAN"	Not Valued
2. 7½% interest in T & C PROPERTIES, a Limited Partnership, evidenced by a written Agreement of August 1, 1967 in which a general partnership known as "ZIFFREN AND ZIFFREN NO. 2" is the general partner, which limited partnership holds real property known as "TOWN AND COUNTRY SHOPPING CENTER" at 3rd and Fairfax, Los Angeles, California	Not Valued
3. 10% interest in "HUNTLEY SANTA MONICA" a partnership evidenced by an "Operating Agreement" of June 20, 1968, under which "ZIFFREN AND ZIFFREN NO. 2" is "Manager", together with an undivided 10% interest in certain improved real property known as "THE HUNTLEY HOUSE" at 111 Second Street, Santa Monica, California	Not Valued
4. 10% interest in L-V PROPERTIES, a partnership evidenced by an "Operating Agreement" of June 26, 1968, under which "ZIFFREN AND ZIFFREN NO. 2" is "Manager", recorded as Document No. 14002 in Book 1519 at Page 614 of Recorder's Office in Solano County, California, together with an undivided 10% interest in certain improved real property known as "LARWIN PLAZA SHOPPING CENTER" Vallejo, California	Not Valued

ITEM	VALUE
5. 14.67% Joint Venture interest in SAHARA SANDS, a partnership in which the operating partner is FRED BARMAN of 9255 West Sunset Boulevard, Los Angeles, California	Not Valued
6. 25% Joint Venture interest in SHADOW PASEO, a partnership in which the operating partner is FRED BARMAN of 9255 West Sunset Boulevard, Los Angeles, California	Not Valued
7. Oil Investment and interest therein, placed with and operated by ROY M. HUFFINTON, INC., of 2210 Tennessee Bldg. Houston, Texas (77002).	Not Valued
8. Cause of action and claim of $250,000.00 against DINO de LAURENTIS CINEMATOGRAFICA, A.P.A and COLUMBIA PICTURES contained in litigation on file in New York Supreme Court wherein Respondent is plaintiff	Not Valued

9. Ownership and/or profit sharing interest and all
   interests and rights in and to a television series
   entitled "THE FUGITIVE" derivative from an Agreement dated November 13, 1962, between Respondent
   and Q.M. Productions, the producers of said series   Not Valued
10. "Residuals" due or to come due from all motion pictures
    and television, or either, which have been completed
    to date in which Respondent participates   Not Valued
11. Ownership and/or profit sharing interests and rights in
    and to a television series entitled "RICHARD DIAMOND" Not Valued
12. Furniture and furnishings formerly in Palm Springs and
    now at Bekins Van & Storage, Beverly Hills, California Not Valued

All tax deductions, benefits or advantages derived from the above
assets are to be divided equally, except future expense deductions which
shall be taken by the party paying same.

(2) TO BE AWARDED PETITIONER

ITEM	VALUE
1. Cash	$ 19,062.55
2. Furniture in Petitioner's apartment at 9255 Doheny Road, Los Angeles, California, known as "Sierra Towers"	8,605.00
3. Prepaid rent and Security Deposit — "Sierra Towers" apartment	1,530.00
4. 1965 Rolls Royce, subject to encumbrance, equity	7,271.80
5. Stock — Ellie Janssen and Associates, Inc., sometimes known as Ellie Janssen Interiors	1.00
6. "RAQUET CLUB" Palm Springs Membership and "FACTORY" Membership	1.00
7. Occidental Life Insurance Policy No. 2634840	21.00
8. North American Life Insurance Policy No. L-574387	1,985.00
9. Occidental Life Insurance Policy No. 4091801	1,000.00
10. Bank Account — ELLIE JANSSEN AND ASSOCIATES, INC.	1,304.12
TOTAL	$ 40,781.47

(3) TO BE AWARDED TO RESPONDENT

ITEM	VALUE
1. Cash	$ 64,232.33

2. Note of TONI K. HOLT secured by Second Deed of Trust
   on Palm Springs Property described as Subleasehold
   estate in and to Lot 3 of Tract 2472 as filed in Book 48,

Page 15 Records of Riverside County, California, dated December 12, 1968 in favor of Petitioner and Respondent in the original sum of $12,200.00	10,277.88
3. Receivable from EXCEDRIN contract due to Respondent	58,500.00
4. Stock in DAVID JANSSEN ENTERPRISES, INC. and D.M.J. ENTERPRISES	1.00
5. Stock in ASTRON PRODUCTIONS, a corporation	1.00
6. Stock in LOS ANGELES AIR TAXI SERVICE, INC., a corporation	1.00
7. AFTRA deposit	5.00
8. Equity in Lot #2 of Tract 2928 as shown by Map on file in Book 52, Pages 46 and 47 of Maps, Riverside County, California, subject to First Deed of Trust, and including plans, blueprints and drawings	31,600.
9. Professional equipment in possession of Respondent	5,212.00
10. Prepaid rent, Respondent's office	515.28
11. Furniture, Respondent's office	3,032.08
12. Equities and all interests in 3 parcels of desert land – Palm Desert, Indian Wells and Thermal, subject to encumbrances thereon	1.00
13. Furniture, furnishings and Spencer Orgell Silver in Respondent's residence	10,322.00
14. Piper Aztec Airplane	33,836.20
15. 1969 Rolls Royce, equity	7,734.00
16. 1965 Travel Lodge trailer	18,000.00
17. Prepaid rent and deposit, Respondent's residence	5,500.00
18. Sovereign Life Insurance Policy #18528	890.00
19. TWA deposit	425.00
20. Tres Vidas Club	5,000.00
21. Tamarisk Country Club	4,800.00
22. All other Club Memberships held by Respondent	1.00
23. Kenya Safari, receivable	1,000.00
24. Los Angeles Air Taxi Service, Inc. receivable	1,697.00
25. A. Shaw, account receivable	500.00
26. Berrere, account receivable	200.00
27. Pete Wilson, account receivable	206.00
28. Astron Productions, account receivable	526.00
TOTAL	$ 264,489.77

XVIII.   To achieve an equal division of community property after payment of debts, Respondent should be ordered to pay and save Petitioner harmless from all of the following community debts and obligations and the follow fees and costs:

ITEM	VALUE
1. Los Angeles Air Taxi Service, Inc.	$ 1,106.19
2. Astron Productions	837.50
3. Sahara Sands	2,273.65
4. City National Bank, Beverly Hills – Note	35,000.00
5. All 1969 Income Taxes, State and Federal (whatever the amount)	1.00
6. All 1970 Income Taxes, State and Federal incurred to date, estimated	100,000.00
7. 1967 and 1968 Federal Income tax liability estimated	50,000.00
8. Eli Parker	2,500.00
9. Dr. Naiditch	1,550.00
10. Pension and Welfare, SAG	6,500.00
11. Sovereign Life Insurance, premium notice	335.84
12. City National Bank, interest on note UF-05812	84.97
13. Magla Productions	113.20
14. Carol Hargreaves	143.00
15. Jona Lingerfelder	53.50
16. Pacific Telephone	87.88
17. Top Hat Cleaners	7.85
18. Wilshire Limo. Service	37.80
19. Huffington Oil charges	19.89
20. Peat, Marwick & Mitchell, additional fees awarded herein	7,350.00
21. Gillen & Scott, attorney fees awarded herein	3,000.00
22. Gillen & Scott, costs awarded herein	98.88
23. Traxler & Raskin, additional attorneys fees awarded herein	30,000.00
24. Traxler & Raskin, costs awarded herein	405.00
TOTAL	$241,506.15

XIX.   Petitioner is entitled to payment forthwith by Respondent of the sum of $19,062.55 (Paragraph XVII(2) which includes the $17,790.15 (Paragraph XII). Respondent is indebted to Petitioner in the sum of $19,062.55, and Petitioner is entitled to Judgment for said amount against Respondent.

XX.   Respondent has the ability to manage, control and settle the claim against DINO de LAURENTIS CINEMATOGRAFICA, S.P.A. and COLUMBIA PICTURES, and he should have the sole authority to do so, subject, however, to the Court's retained and continued jurisdiction to value and equally divide all benefits received therefrom. All costs and expenses of the court action concerning said claim, including attorneys' fees, can and should be borne by Respondent, since he has the financial ability to do so, subject to a deduction of one-half (1/2) thereof from Petitioner's share of the benefits.

XXI.   The Court can and should retain jurisdiction to equally divide the furniture formerly in the Palm Springs home, and now in storage at Bekins Van & Storage in Beverly Hills, California, if the parties are unable to do so.

XXII.   Each party can and should sign and turn over to the other any document requested by the other to effectuate the terms of the Judgment.

CONCLUSIONS OF LAW

XXIII.   An INTERLOCUTORY JUDGMENT OF DISSOLUTION should be awarded petitioner.

XXIV.   A DECREE OF NULLITY should not be granted.

XXV.   Community Property, after deducting debts, should be ordered equally divided as provided above.

XXVI.   Support for Petitioner, and payable by Respondent, should be ordered as provided above.

XXVII.   Petitioner's legal fees and costs, and accounting fees, should be ordered paid by Respondent as provided above.

XVIII.   JUDGMENT should be signed and entered in accordance with the FINDINGS OF FACT AND CONCLUSIONS OF LAW.

Dated: *August 27, 1970*

Richard L. Wells
_____
RICHARD L. WELLS
JUDGE OF THE SUPERIOR COURT

APPENDIX II
Last Will and Testament

LAST WILL AND TESTAMENT

OF

DAVID JANSSEN

I, DAVID JANSSEN, a resident of Los Angeles County, State of California, declare this to be my Last Will and Testament and revoke all former Wills and Codicils to Wills.

1. DECLARATIONS

I declare that I am married, that my wife's name is DANI JANSSEN, also known as DARLYNE JANSSEN, and that I have never had any children. My wife has one child by a former marriage, namely, her daughter, DEBORAH GUTERMUTH.

2. DEBTS AND EXPENSES

I direct my Executor to pay all of my just debts, funeral expenses and administration expenses from my general estate as soon after my death as conveniently can be done. This provision shall not be mandatory upon my Executor with respect to any secured debts on property belonging to my estate, and my Executor shall use his best judgment as to whether, when and to what extent such secured debts shall be discharged out of my estate.

3. PROPERTY

It is my intention hereby to dispose of all real and personal property which I have the right to dispose of my Will, including my separate property and my share of the community property acquired by my wife, DANI, and me during our marriage.

4. DISTRIBUTION OF ESTATE

I give, devise and bequeath all of my estate to my wife, DANI, provided that she survives me by five (5) months. If my wife shall predecease me or fails to survive me by five (5) months, I give, devise and bequeath all of my estate to my wife's daughter, DEBORAH GUTERMUTH.

5. TAXES

I direct that all estate and inheritance taxes payable by reason of my death (without limitation to taxes attributable to property passing under this Will, or any other limitation) shall be paid out of the residue of my estate and shall not be charged against or collected from any legatee, devisee or beneficiary or any other transferee or beneficiary of property included in my gross taxable estate.

145

6. HEIRS

Except as otherwise provided in this Will, I have intentionally and with full knowledge omitted to provide for my heirs.

7. CONTEST

If any devisee, legatee or beneficiary named in this Will, or any person who would be entitled to share in my estate through intestate succession, shall in any manner whatsoever, either directly or indirectly, oppose, contest or attack this Will, or the distribution of my estate hereunder, or seek to impair, invalidate or set aside any of the provisions of this Will, or shall aid in doing any of the above acts, then in that event I hereby give and bequeath to any such person the sum of One Dollar ($1.00) only in lieu of any other share or interest in my estate, either under this Will or through intestate succession.

8. INTEREST

No interest shall be paid on any legacy or bequest given under this Will or any Codicil to it.

9. Executor

9.1 Appointment

I appoint my friend, KENNETH ZIFFREN, as Executor hereunder. In the event KENNETH ZIFFREN shall be unable or unwilling to serve or to continue to serve as Executor hereunder, I appoint PAUL ZIFFREN to serve in his stead. In the event PAUL ZIFFREN shall be unable or unwilling to serve as successor Executor hereunder, I appoint CITY NATIONAL BANK, a national banking association, Beverly Hills, California (or its successors by merger, consolidation or otherwise) to serve as Executor hereunder.

9.2 Bond

No Executor appointed by me hereunder shall be required to post bond.

9.3 Sale

I authorize my Executors to sell, lease or encumber my mortgage, deed of trust or otherwise, the whole or any part of my estate, with or without notice, and at public or private sale. I further direct that my Executors may at their option continue to hold, manage and operate any property or business that I may own or hold at the time of my death, the profits or losses, if any, to inure to or be chargeable against my estate and not to my said Executors.

9.4 Partition

I authorize my Executors, on any preliminary or final distribution of the property in my estate, to partition, allot and distribute my estate in kind, including undivided interests in my estate or any part of it, or partly in cash and partly in kind, or entirely in cash, in my Executor's absolute discretion and at valuations determined by my Executors.

9.5 Investment

I authorize my Executors to invest any surplus monies in their hands during the period of probate in any investment which men of prudence, discretion and intelligence acquire for their own account. Without limiting the generality of the foregoing, my Executors may invest such surplus monies in corporate obligations of every kind, stocks, preferred or common, shares of investment trusts, investment companies and mutual funds and mortgage participations.

10. PARTIAL INVALIDITY

Should any part, clause, provision or condition of this Will be held to be void, invalid and inoperative, then I direct that such invalidity shall not affect any other clause, provision or condition hereof; but the remainder of this Will shall be effective as though such clauses, provisions or conditions had not been contained herein.

11. CONSTRUCTION

11.1 Number and Gender

Wherever I have used the word "Executors" in this Will, it shall include all numbers and genders.

11.2 Captions

Paragraph headings are for ease of reference only and shall not affect the construction of this Will.

IN WITNESS WHEREOF, I have hereunto subscribed my name this 24 day of *February*, 1977.

The foregoing instrument, consisting of five (5) pages, including this page, was at the date hereof, by DAVID JANSSEN, signed as and declared to be his Will, in the presence of us who, at his request and in his presence, and in the presence of each other have subscribed our names as witnesses thereto. Each of us observed the signing of this Will by DAVID JANSSEN and by each other subscribing witness and knows that each signature is the true signature of the person whose name was signed.

Each of us is now more than twenty-one (21) years of age and a competent witness and resides at the address set forth after his name.

We are acquainted with DAVID JANSSEN. At this time, he is over the age of eighteen (18) years, and to the best of our knowledge he is of sound mind and is not acting under duress, menace, fraud, misrepresentation or undue influence.

We declare under penalty of perjury that the foregoing is true and correct.

Executed on *February 24*, 1977, at Los Angeles, California.

Appendix III
An Episode Synopsis

Episode air date: TV's _The Fugitive_ 10/22/63

Decision in the Ring—#4601

Joe Smith, a Negro fighter, is willing to sacrifice his sanity and possibly, his life, for recognition as a "first-class citizen" in the ring rather than a second-class citizen in the medical profession. Joe's wife, Laura, accepts his decision but regrets he has turned his back on medicine.

Richard Kimble, alias Ray Miller, a fugitive wrongly convicted of murdering his wife, works as cut-man for Joe, a middleweight contender for the championship. During their weeks in training, a series of incidents reveals to Kimble, a doctor until his trial and conviction, that Joe is suffering from serious brain damage — enough to threaten his mental balance or life. Kimble alone shares this secret with Joe. Despite his attempts to get the fighter to leave the ring, Joe deliberately chooses to pursue his fight career since his previous efforts to be a doctor met with painful discouragement and a lowered status.

Unknown to cut-man Kimble, he has been in jeopardy of exposure from the start when Boxing Commissioner Murphy —an ex-reporter who earlier exposed Joe's manager, Lou Bragan, as a crooked operator — assigns plainclothesman Henry Stone to stick close and fingerprint all members of the training party, including Kimble.

At the Sports Arena, before the fight, Laura senses danger for Joe and pleads with Kimble to help her. Kimble suggests that the only way to make Joe stop fighting is to force him to make a choice between

Laura and the ring. Laura packs her bags to leave. She tells Joe she's not running out on him but going home until he comes to his senses and quits. Joe is adamant — he'll fight.

Minutes before the main bout, Murphy gets an identification on Kimble and surrounds the arena with police. Joe lies to protect Kimble from apprehension, realizing he is a fugitive and a doctor trying desperately to regain his own status in life. This fundamental kinship between them makes such an impression on Joe that he decides to reveal his brain injury to the doctors, thus ending his career in the ring.

Kimble succeeds in escaping, reads the news on the road and takes satisfaction in having saved Joe's life and restored him to the medical profession.

David Janssen
Fan Clubs

At the most recent "Fans of the Fugitive" Convention, which is held annually at the Radisson Hollywood Roosevelt Hotel (7000 Hollywood Boulevard, Hollywood, CA 90028, 1-800-950-7667), I was delighted to meet David's fans from all over the world. I especially thank the following for their continuing efforts on behalf of all David Janssen's fans. They can be reached at:

DAVID BROWN
Fans of the Fugitive
511 Stillmeadow
Richardson, Texas 75081
(214) 669-9388

BOB REINHARDT
Editor
"The Stafford Chronicle"
6500 Brush Country Road
Austin, Texas 78749-1403
(512) 476-5957

RUSTY POLLARD
Editor
"On the Run"
P.O. Box 461402
Garland, Texas 75046
(214) 272-2633

CATHERINE ROBERT
President
"The Stafford Club"
83 Rue Pasteur
5400 Nancy
France, Europe